SITTING WITH SPIRITS

SITTING WITH SPIRITS

Exploring the Unseen World
in the Margins of Christianity

Bob Doto

New Old Traditions

Thank you to everyone who was willing to read over early versions of this work, even when I would send newer, "cleaner," versions a day later (esp. Anna, Tiffany, and Mallorie). Special thanks to Michael and Sophia for the support, inspo, and shares. An extra special thank you to Becky for workshopping the ideas in this book, late into the evening, when all you really wanted to do was sleep.

First Edition: May 2020
Printed in the United States of America
ISBN-13: 978-1-64858-219-6

Cover image and interior artwork: Ellen Harling
@ellenharlingillustration "Illustrations of spirits inhabiting ancient Roman urns"

CONTENTS

Sitting with Spirits *is excerpted from a longer work exploring liminal, shadowy, and magical entry points into the Christ tradition.*

In this excerpt I have attempted to show that having a relationship with the world of spirits is not only possible within the Catholic and Christian traditions, but also inherent. To that end, this short work explores the concepts of both "spirit" and "spirit work" through the lens of biblical hermeneutics, magical and mindfulness practices, shadow work, and self-inquiry.

As with all my writing on the subject, I hope to depict a Christ tradition that looks nothing like what we've seen. And, everything like what we've dreamed.

To my mom.
My first ancestor.

God is a spirit; and those who worship God must worship in both spirit and truth.
—John 4:24

Chapter 1
Bombing

THE ENTRANCE was located on an empty block running alongside a maintenance yard for ailing subway cars. A cat bent its body around the post of a collapsing fence, while city busses sped up and down the main drag hidden behind a row of houses across the street. Nothing around me suggested there was a rosary taking place that night. No sign. No people. No smell of copal. Just an unmarked metal door behind a partially opened steel guard gate.

Thirty seconds after texting my contact to let her know I had made it, but clueless as to how to get in, a woman poked her head out of the door, and waved me inside.

Fernando greeted me with a big smile the moment I landed at the bottom of the stairs. He yelled to someone in the back room. "Lupe!" A woman in her thirties walked up and shook my hand, kissing me on either cheek. Out from behind her stepped a young boy who couldn't have been more than eight years old. He wore thick eyeglasses, begrudgingly peeled from the saccharine-colored cartoon streaming on his smartphone. He reached out his hand. Fernando, looking proud, said, "This is Nelson."

I was met with a very polite, very novice handshake. "It's nice to meet you, Nelson."

"He'll be your translator tonight."

IT WAS 7PM. I was standing in the basement of a hardware store brightly lit with long fluorescent lights attached to the ceiling. About twenty people were sitting in a large circle on various benches made out of wood planks balanced on buckets, empty milk crates, and coolers filled with water and beer. It was early in the winter months, but it was getting late in the evening, and the temperature outside had dropped considerably since the afternoon. The cement floor radiated the cold from the hard earth below. Even with shoes on my toes cramped and cracked like a frozen pond.

I arrived thinking I was attending a public rosary to Santa Muerte, the popular folk saint whose "come as you are" attitude had endeared me and about ten million other people into offering monthly devotions. Her popularity had skyrocketed since the early 2000s, due in part to her accepting nature, especially toward those whom the Church had cast aside. For Santa Muerte, if you had any plans on dying at some point, then she was your godmother. It didn't matter where you came from or what you wore.

So, it surprised me that night when I found myself in a room full of people dressed in varying approximations of white from head to toe. Not a strand of rosary beads in sight. I took out my ratty book of crosswords, and sat on a wooden box against the wall, thinking of five-letter words for "cheese choice."

AT ABOUT 9:30PM two people sat down on either side of a rectangle table at the front of the circle. Fernando sat on the left wearing grey sweatpants and a white t-shirt. An elderly woman named, Conchi, sat on the right wearing a frilly white skirt, resting her chin on her hands gripping the top of a wooden cane balanced between her legs.

The ceremony, which I was quickly coming to realize was not going to be a rosary, began with a short talk on the order of events. Both Fernando and Conchi spoke of the possible physical experiences we might have, reminding us that these were totally normal, and to remain calm. This was followed by a litany of prayers, which eventually blended into songs sung call and response. From there, things moved quickly.

Conchi was the only person who entered into possession that night. With each new song we sang, her body contorted to accommodate the transformation taking place within her. Then the healings started.

I never got the name of the spirit Conchi was

in contact with, but it seemed to be having a good time, feeding off the attention. We all watched as the spirit called people out on this unhealthy behavior or that truth told slant. Some she berated at great length. *You need to stop texting that other woman! Pay attention to your family!* Others got off easy. *Your grandmother is watching over you. She want's coffee. Bring her some coffee.* She called specific people to the front of the room, had them kneel, and removed whatever malicious force had been making problems for them. The assistants would set fires on the concrete floor with lighter fluid. Spray a line of the stuff up the stairs and out the door. Chopping at it with a machete. Chasing the spirit out of the room. Conchita would query the attendees when they were done. *Who's got a mother that's sick? Who's got a business that's hurting? Whose husband is being inappropriate with the neighbor's wife?* Some she would hit with white flowers, the stems and petals getting stuck in their jeans and hair. Most people got a mouthful of rum sprayed in their face.

This went on for hours, and at some point I noticed that many of the children had either drifted off to sleep, or were in the beginning stages of self-induced smartphone comas.

It was during one of these scans of the room that I noticed people's faces turn toward mine. I immediately thought I was about to be chastised for not paying attention, when Lupe tapped my hand saying, "Padrino wants to speak to you."

I peered up toward the front, and saw Fernando looking at me. "I have something I want to ask you, Bob." I looked around, and watched as a dozen or so people turned back to face me.

It seemed moments earlier Conchi had received a vision about my coming to the circle, and both her and Fernando needed to first clarify a few things. He looked at me saying, "This may be a bit personal, ok?"

"Ok," I said. I knew enough about séances and spirit work in general to know that the spirits liked to get personal. Messages might involve a family member or an ex-lover trying to get back at you. But, I was new. So, I didn't expect much.

"I don't want to offend you or anything."

I nodded saying that it was cool. "Ask whatever you want."

"Ok," he said. "Are you gay?"

It was literally the last question I expected him to ask, but there it was. The people sitting closest to me looked as if I had just been asked my shoe size. I was taken aback, but also felt a bit angry. Had I had any sense at the time, I might have postured my most righteous self, questioning the question. *Why is my, or anyone else's sexuality being put on trial? Why does it matter who a person has sex with? God doesn't care about who you love. Sexuality is a spectrum. Gender is a construct.* If I was feeling spicy, I might have thrown something in there about intersectionality. Everyone would have stood up and cheered. The young people in attendance would have lifted me up on their shoulders and carried me into the street, where we would have reclaimed the block for the liberation of sexual identities. It would have been a good day for social justice.

But, instead I just responded in the negative. "No, I'm not gay."

"It's ok either way," he said. "We just needed to know."

It was my first time sitting with this circle, and the question confirmed that, yes, I had absolutely no idea what was going on.

WHEN I FIRST ARRIVED, Fernando told me he could see a large spirit following me in the room. He remarked how it stood behind me, big, potent, and protective. I, of course, had no idea what "potent" meant given the circumstances, and certainly had no knowledge of what that could mean within the context of the rosary I thought I was attending.

After asking about my sexuality, Conchi said something in Spanish, which I missed. Fernando looked at her and shrugged his shoulders, turning back toward me. "Are you sure your spirit doesn't have anything to offer us?" I was caught by the sudden shift in the questioning, and looked for clues on people's faces as to what I might have missed. "It's ok. Everyone here understands English." A number of attendees nodded. "I can see your spirit wants to speak," he said. "It needs to speak. You have to let it out. What does it have to say?"

I looked down at my upturned hands resting on my legs, trying to reorganize, and catch up to this new round of questioning. *Ok. What does my big potent spirit have to say*? I started to feel anxious. I felt the tell-tale signs of both spirit possession and a panic attack. *Pleeease don't be a panic attack*. The hair was rising on the back of my neck, and a tingling sensation quickly crept along my limbs. I realized there were things I wanted to say, but felt uncomfortable doing so. *The old lady has knee problems. That woman with the blue hair. Something about her windows. Fernando needs to not get a big head. That kid needs to stop taking drugs. That man's hiding his sexua....* Wait.... It was maddening. Were these my personal thoughts, or were they communications from spirit? Or, were these just projections? Was it ok to have opinions about people I had never met? This conundrum had come up a dozens of times before. And, here it was again. Confusing me. Causing me to doubt myself.

One thing I could rely on was my body. The confirmation of the physical sensations I was having were slowly starting to overtake my rational thinking mind. My body began to feel as if it was not entirely my own. I wanted my thoughts to tease out from one another. But, they didn't. I took an inhale, and lifted my head, holding the breath in my lungs slightly. *Trust it*, I thought to myself. *Trust what you're getting.*

I exhaled long and slow, gathering the courage to tell a handful of strangers personal things I might hesitate to tell my own friends. I smiled, and locked eyes with Roberto. With a slightly embarrassed form of broken Spanish, I pulled what I could from my "big, potent" spirit. "I'm sorry," I said. "I don't have anything to say."

The people around me looked to the floor and then back to Fernando. Conchi was eyeing me. Fernando rubbed his large hands along his thighs a few times, pausing to pick something off the fabric. He rubbed it between his fingers, and flicked it onto the floor. "That's ok," he said. "Maybe next time."

MY GRAND ENTRANCE into the practice of *misa espiritual,* the Latin American branch of spiritualism in the Americas, felt like a bust. My performance deflated. For ten years I had haunted every *botanica* in New York City, the one-stop spiritual shops spread throughout urban areas across the United States catering to the needs of Latin Americans. I even went as far as to visit every one in a single weekend. At the time there were upwards of a hundred dotting the five boroughs. I made it to seven.

Ten years looking for a way into the seemingly secret world of Lucumi spirituality. Ten years pestering shop owners about what this candle meant or that floor wash did. Ten years wishing a *babalawo* or *oba*, the high officiants of the faith, would endear to my curiosity, and invite me into their world. Ten years later, here I was, having accidentally stumbled upon the Lucumi religion in all its magical glory, and I was bombing.

Throughout those ten years I read every book I could afford on the Lucumi religion. The books I couldn't afford—the many that were out of print, and costing hundreds of dollars—I would read snippets of online where I could find them. I took a special interest in the practices associated with the *espiritismo* wing of the faith, which, at the time, sounded like a séance on thirty hits of acid.

The prosperity-centric spiritualist culture I was familiar with seemed tame in comparison. The few services I had previously attended focused mainly on the subject of wealth, and how to get it, peppered with a bit of "I feel spirits in this room" talk. The services offered $20 séances to attendees who wished to stay after hours. I felt very little in the way of spirits at these meetings, and usually left feeling bored; happy to have had the experience, glad to know this or that spirit was wishing me good fortune, but always wondering why they seemed so vague.

Espiritismo was different. Healings happened

in the moment. Spiritual barriers were exposed on the cold floor, soaked with lighter fluid, covered in mysterious markings made with white *cascarilla* chalk. Received messages weren't for you to take home and meditate on. They were meant to be enacted right then and there. Got a problem? Get on your knees and let's take care of it.

Espiritismo felt like the right counterbalance to my otherwise solitary yogic practices. It also felt like another back door into the Catholic religion of my upbringing, a religion I had long abandoned, but was desperate to re-engage with. Santa Muerte had brought me indoors many years prior. Lucumi and espiritismo felt like secret rooms hidden in the back of closets. I knew espiritismo wasn't the spiritual practice of my ancestors—I'm Italian-American, and espiritismo is decidedly Afro-Caribbean—but, in my mind it was a step in the right direction. Something about romance languages, saints, and a shared appreciation of street festivals.

For ten years I read. And, through reading I came to believe. I believed in the existence of spirits. I believed you could communicate with the unseen world. I believed in the Lucumi religion of which espiritismo was an integral part. And, through this belief, I believed more and more that the religion of my parents could become my own once again. After all, many *espiritistas* remained devout Catholics. Maybe I too could be a Catholic.

Of course, my Catholicism wasn't going to be the Catholicism of the Church. That bloated institution had abandoned me and many others long ago. No. My Catholicism was going to be a Catholicism with spirit. One Holy Spirit and many human spirits.

But, there in Fernando's basement I was stuck. I had no spirit to call my own. It was all too clear that books and believing had only taken me so far. I was at the door. Hell, I was inside sitting at the kids table elbowing an eight-year-old boy every five minutes to translate what the adults were talking about. I was physically inside. But, spiritually, I felt far from home.

Chapter 2

Orientation

Beliefs Make the Magic

At its most basic, spirit work can be defined as the practice of engaging with the spirits of people who have died. It's a simple enough definition, and one I use whenever the situation calls for something succinct.

I came to Fernando's with this definition already tucked away in the back of my mind. I also came with twenty five years of spiritual exploration under my belt. To be safe I brought a few visualization exercises to orient my thoughts, some yogic breathing practices to quiet my mind, a string of rosary beads to pray on, and a belief that with a quiet mind one could communicate with the dead. I thought that would suffice. But, when asked what the dead had to say, I had nothing to offer.

SPIRT WORK is an incredibly varied practice. No two cultures do it the same. In fact, no two traditions in the *same culture* do it the same. Beliefs differ across traditions, and beliefs determine the practice.

Whenever we enter a new spiritual community, we enter this world of beliefs. We may think we're there to learn how to set up the altar, when to bow, and what to wear. But, that's only part of it. Fernando asked me to speak, because in his tradition it's believed that spirits make themselves known, in part, through the voice. In espiritismo, we speak our spirits into being.

But, this isn't how all spirits play the game. Compare espiritismo to the way in which Classical Chinese Medicine works with spirits. The Five Spirits known as the Shen, Zhi, Yi, Po, and Hun manifest as disturbances in the body-mind. Most of their behaviors would be unrecognizable to the non-believer. Out of the five, only the Hun would show up on a Westerner's radar, who will typically expect a spirit to be preoccupied with creeping around the apartment. The Hun isn't creepy. But, it does hover over your bed while you sleep. Rarely, however, is there a need to call on the Hun or any of the other spirits to speak aloud. They exist in the context of physical and mental health, managed through medical interventions involving herbs, acupuncture, and massage therapy.

Mediumship in the United States couldn't look more different. In Chinese medicine the Five Spirits are believed to be aspects of a person's internal makeup, usually in need of balance. Western séances are intended to pass along information and guidance from an outside source. The

Five Spirits are diagnosed through assessing patterns in a person's demeanor and overall health by a doctor of Chinese medicine. In séances, the spirits often do the diagnosing.

But, it doesn't stop there. Examples of belief determining practice abound. We see possession taking place in traditions where spirits are believed to interact with humanity through the use of human vessels. We come across jars of cemetery dirt in traditions that believe the dead communicate through earth matter. Incense is used when there's a belief that spirits are attracted to the smell; candles when spirits are believed to feast on the light.

When we come to spirit work believing in the existence of spirits, but without actual beliefs in how they behave, we're like toddlers watching adults speak, but unable to do so ourselves. We can make ourselves known through various sounds, but have few resources for getting specific about what we want.

The truth is, once you begin scratching the surface, it becomes increasingly difficult to talk about what spirit work is, because, what it is, is determined by what gets done. And, what gets done changes from culture to culture.

The Spirit in the Work

In the West, the word "spirit" connotes breath, breathing, and vitality. From the Latin *spiritus*, "spirit" is the etymological basis of the word "inspiration." To be inspired is to be invigorated with spirit, to be full of life, to have spirit breathed into you as good thoughts. In this way, the spirit of a person might be thought of as the motivating energetic force within every human being. The thing that gives life. From a theological perspective, it is the aspect of ourselves that was given to us through God having breathed life into the first human.

When we talk about spirit in the biblical sense, we're really talking about two things at the same time: the Holy Spirit and the human spirit. As will be shown later, the Holy Spirit needs to be gifted, either by the grace of God, or by being in the company of those who've already had the pleasure. So, while the Holy Spirit may be God's gift to humanity through the ascension of Jesus Christ, it's still a gift that needs to be given.

But, the Holy Spirit is not the only spirit mentioned in the Bible. A plurality of spirits can be found around every corner in the New Testament. The epistles, written by some of the earliest members of the forming Christ community, made explicit statements about both "testing the spirits" (plural), as well as how to best manage situations when more than one person was being possessed by spirits (again, plural). Jesus repeatedly removes impure spirits (plural) from people, while Paul states that one of the gifts of the Holy Spirit is the ability to distinguish between spirits (again, plural).

In biblical times, it was accepted that the human spirit was separate from the human body, able to exist independently after the body expired.[1] Today, the idea is suspect. But, for those who still believe that spirit exists *ever-so-slightly* independent of the physical form that houses it, it may not be so difficult to imagine. If the life of the host is somehow cut short, as with a so-called untimely death, the spirit may continue to exist. Perhaps, out of sheer momentum. Perhaps, out of a need to tend to unfinished business.

It seems easy enough to accept. And yet, the idea that we can actually *communicate* with the spirit of someone who has died, can be hard to swallow. For many people, the concept of an "invisible world" is simply unacceptable. Most people who have an appreciation of something unseen in their midst, still save space in the back of their minds for doubt. Which is understandable.

Despite its rich history of spiritualists, Holy Ghost preachers, ecstatic millenarianists, and second coming prophetesses,[2] contemporary US culture does not prioritize spirit. It prioritizes self-determination. The United States is founded on the idea that if you want something to be a certain way, you need to make that change yourself. No otherworldly power is going to help you. Seeing as the United States is considered one of the more religious countries in the world,[3] one might think that religiosity would translate into a belief in intercession from the unseen world. But, divine intervention tends to take a back seat in capitalist societies.

And yet, even our own largely materialist culture has a place set aside for things unseen. It's not uncommon to hear someone say that an exceptional person's "spirit lives on," or that a person has "the spirit of a lion." Perhaps you've been told by someone that you have your mother or father's spirit. All of these statements, as passing and unconscious as they may be, are a testament to a time when something ethereal existed in our midst. So, while secular society's conception of spirit may be nostalgic and vague, it does have an appreciation of a certain *something* that at one time traversed the chasm between self and other, a cursory understanding that something non-material once upon a time made its way from one entity into another.

Left within the confines of passing conversation, however, spirit tends to evaporate into the background. Spirit, if believed in at all these days, reads as a curiosity at best. It's only when we start to intentionally engage the "spirit that lives on" that we begin to feel that these aspects of people passed are here now, both as entities to communicate with, as well as potential allies on our spiritual journey.

Community or Commodity?

> *In America nothing reaches the media unless it's commodification. This is all the media is interested in, something which can sell products.*
> —Hakim Bey, *Millenium*

The idea that spirit lives among us has been knocking on our door for some time now. Over the past twenty years there has been a surge of interest in all things spiritual, and in that time interest in traditional Western expressions has steadily grown. People have started reclaiming traditional practices associated with witchcraft, ancestral veneration, herbalism, and astrology, and the repurposing of Mary as the Divine Mediatrix Mother continues to inspire new devotees.

Up until a few years ago, there would have been very little room for the Holy Spirit in our very hip spiritual climate. While interest in the biblical tradition, especially in its magical and folk elements, seems to have grown at an increasingly rapid rate, among pagans, witches and occultists with an interest in Catholic magic there is still an understandable hesitancy to keep anything seeming "too Christian" at arm's length. In cases where an interest in the Christian tradition has sprung up, it has almost always been in it's hybrid and syncretic magical and folk expressions. For progressive young Americans interested in Western spirituality, the Bible, and the religion tethered to it, still presents as a significant problem.

Left-leaning antagonism toward a State increasingly enamored with far-right takes on "Christian mores," has put many progressive-minded spiritual seekers in a tricky spot. Do you reject your culture's religious expression, and orient yourself within a spirituality towing less baggage? Or, do you climb inside, and root out what speaks to you, reclaiming what is rightfully yours? Even though new books and blogs are being written all the time, it's a question that increasingly gets answered on social media through the sharing of memes, photos of home altars, and pithy affirmations.

Social media has allowed people from different parts of the world to share their personal practices and reclamations of the faith. People with heterodox takes on traditional exegesis are finding it easier to connect with like-minded individuals and groups. There is a sense that a magical Catholic surge is manifesting just over the horizon.

And yet, social media has also turned expressions of spirituality into fodder for late-stage capitalist branding. People document their spiritual practice not only for networking purposes, but also in the hopes of legitimizing the monetization of their magical offerings, usually at an inflated price point.

A platform like Instagram, which has been accepted by many self-styled spiritual radicals as a necessity, transforms posts into products. Images of candle magic double as advertisements for candle magic. A post about spiritism, becomes an ad for spirit consultations. If there's an actual business tied to the account, the currency exchanged may be monetary. But, as is so often the case, the currency is merely egoic, a currency of "Likes" conveniently interpreted as "affirmations." In an ironic twist, in the realm of social media, those who posture as being the most anti-orthodox and, as is the flavor of the day, anti-capitalist, are sometimes the most spiritually materialistic of all, many following in the footsteps of the hippies of the 1960s who, by the 1980s, had morphed into stock market yuppies, recontextualizing anti-government sentiment as anti-government oversight.

From a financial standpoint, it's not surprising to see why. The yoga industry alone, which through the late 1990s and early 2000s paved the way for our current state of hyper-capitalist spirituality, is an $80 billion dollar industry, just shy of all the wealth in Europe.[4] If something which was once the primary practice of hermits living in caves can be turned into a multibillion dollar industry, maybe something called "folk Catholicism" can be too! After all, spiritism and witchcraft have already begun to merge with slogan-forward pop psychology, taking cues from the fandom success of Instagram self-help gurus parading as therapists.

But, does the value of the spiritual market, the number of memes being shared on social media, or the branding of expensive takes on inherently inexpensive spiritual practices have anything whatsoever to do with spirituality? Are we actually living in a spiritually woke time?

Old-Timey Holy Ghost Spirituality

The biblical world was rife with spirit. The stuff was everywhere. Spirits began their lives inside humans, fawn, and fauna, but when their hosts passed away or dried up, they found new places to hide. They spread out, seeping into every available nook and cranny. In an effort to establish some sense of sanity, idols, cemeteries, and shrines were set up as domiciles for these wayfaring entities. The hope was that they'd behave and stay put. But, this was rarely the case. Spirits would regularly escape, and latch on to unwitting people. Those who could handle the stowaways would go on to become inspired prophets and poets. Others would simply go mad.

SPIRITS no longer cause people to go mad. These days, madness is seen as an unfortunate psychological glitch, an inability to distinguish between reality and fantasy due to chemical imbalances, drug use, or emotional trauma. Even "inspiration," a word embodied with spirit, is less an expression of the ephemeral, and more the logical outcome of putting oneself in the right place at the right time, followed by a series of ah-ha moments.

Spirit and spirituality typically play little to no role in either. Inspiration and madness have become too messy for spirituality's very tailored persona. Today's spirituality is rational and "grounded." It's sensible and "engaged." It's there when you need it. Happy to sit quietly in the corner if you don't. You can invite it over for dinner, and it'll never overstay its welcome. Spirituality is respectful that way.

Two thousand years ago the spirits were a downright nuisance. They caused people to get sick, have a run of bad luck, rant and rave in the middle of the street, go mute, blind, or worse.

So, while we may think of ourselves and our boutique apothecaries and nuanced appreciations of subtle energies as being spiritually evolved, one could argue that biblical times, rooted in direct experiences of the Spirit *in everyday life*, were even more spiritually-conscious, dare I say, more spiritual, than we are today.

Today, the word "spiritual" means so many things that at times it can be hard to know if it means anything at all. Being a "spiritual person" usually refers to someone who believes in a higher power, but does not necessarily align with any one particular religion, the oft-repeated phrase "I'm spiritual, but not religious" acting as a sort of unofficial declaration of faith. But, the term could just as well refer to a person who does not believe in a higher power at all, but appreciates that there is more to life than what we see. By contrast, being a spiritual person could also mean not believing in a higher power, not believing in anything existing outside apparent reality, not believing in anything one might consider to be even particularly "spiritual," but holding a special place in one's heart for the idea that love connects all beings.

No matter where a person falls on the spiritual spectrum, being a spiritual person today is an expression of belief. It is something you ultimately chose to be.

This, however, is not how the term "spiritual" would have been understood two thousand years ago. To be considered a spiritual person in biblical times had very little to do with how you defined yourself or how frequently you meditated. To be spiritual would have meant that you were in direct communication with the Spirit of God. It would have meant that this Spirit had come into your midst, and that you were displaying the very visible effects of that Spirit's presence.

Jesus' followers would have agreed with this understanding of the term "spiritual," albeit with one *very* important caveat. In his massive work, *The Holy Spirit*, Anthony C. Thistelton discusses the Apostle Paul, and his understanding of the term "spiritual," which would ultimately shape Christian belief for thousands of years. To Paul, whether a person was spiritual or not was entirely dependent on a person's relationship to the Spirit of God, what he and his comrades called "the Holy Spirit," *as it was specifically promised by Jesus Christ.* Whether or not you meditated had nothing to do with it. Thistelon states that Paul's usage of the Greek word *pneumatikos*, or "spiritual," in his letters "is alluding specifically to the agency, work, and effects of the *Holy Spirit*," and that when Paul uses the same term in reference to a "spiritual person," he is referring "to those whose life and thought are characterized by Holy Spirit." Even Paul's usage of *pneumatika*, which Thistelton defines as "spiritual things," is said to be Paul's way of describing "spiritual truths which the Holy Spirit reveals and imparts."[5]

To Paul it didn't matter if you chose to believe in love or alternate realities. It didn't matter if you identified as spiritual rather than religious. Far from being either a statement of belief regarding a person's outlook on life or a choice one makes to become more peaceful and calm, to be a spiritual person meant you were in direct communion with the Holy Spirit, as promised by Jesus Christ, as gifted by God.

Today, our modern sensibilities are quick to inform us that Paul's take on spirituality is incredibly limited. To see spirituality as valid only in cases where a specifically Christian Holy Spirit has made itself known, in a world made up of multiple religious expressions, is to be spiritually imperialistic at best. At worst, fascistic.

But, perhaps there is something to be gained from Paul's narrow take. Perhaps learning how the ancients engaged with spirits, how they defined "spiritual," and how both might translate into living an inspired life today can help orient our practice. Perhaps, by framing what we believe in the historical beliefs of our spiritual tradition, we can better understand what it is we're actually doing when we engage the unseen world, and for what reason. Perhaps, as is so often the case, we need to look back in order to move forward.

Chapter 3
Holy Spirit

But the Advocate, the Holy Spirit, whom the Father will send in my name, will teach you all things and will remind you of everything I have said to you.

—John 14:26

THERE WAS A TIME when I assumed spirit was intangible, spread out, and diffuse. If I was able to conceptualize it at all, Spirit would have been boundaryless and indifferent. Even the Catholic tradition I was raised in referred to the Holy Spirit as less a "thing" to be actively engaged with, and more an idea, a concept used to round out the various qualities of a God who was said to be both intelligent and embodied in Jesus Christ.

Not until I began unpacking what the Bible actually said about the Holy Spirit, did I realize that, far from being some loosely defined energetic presence or theological tool, the Holy Spirit, and, by extension, spirits in general, were positively confrontational. Not in a negative, aggressive sense. But, in the sense that one could confront or be confronted by either. Neither were passive.

Learning to appreciate how the Holy Spirit functions in the Bible was fundamental to my appreciation of spirit work both in general and as it exists within the context of the Christ tradition.

By using the Bible as a guidebook, a literal "spirit manual," I became familiar with the earliest examples of how Spirit engaged with the mystics who came before me, and how it might engage with me today. Cultivating a relationship with the Holy Spirit informed how I interacted with the world and the spirits who make up such an integral part of it.

As is the case with most things learned from history, story is where I encountered much of these teachings.

Pentecost

While certainly not the first account of the Holy Spirit in the New Testament, the story of Pentecost is one of the most explicit.

Pentecost celebrates a day in biblical history when many of Jesus' disciples and followers, having gathered in Jerusalem for the harvest festival, were taken, possessed by, or otherwise overcome with the Holy Spirit. Among the stated one hundred twenty people present were Mary, Jesus' mother; "a number of women" among whom commentators have included Mary Magdalene,

Salome, Susanna, Joanna, Mary and Martha of Bethany;[6] as well as Jesus' remaining eleven male disciples: "Peter, John, James and Andrew; Philip and Thomas, Bartholomew and Matthew; James son of Alphaeus and Simon the Zealot, and Judas son of James."[7] Judas Iscariot, who had hung himself out of guilt for his betrayal of Jesus, was the only well-known disciple not present.

The term Pentecost comes from the Greek "fiftieth" and refers to the fifty days between the end of Passover and the Feast of the Harvest, today a Jewish holiday known as "Shavuot." The Feast of the Harvest was a major celebration and involved a pilgrimage to the Temple where Jews would bring offerings of the first harvested wheat. Jesus' earliest disciples, being Jewish, would have been at the Temple as part of this celebration. And, it was in this joyous environment that they were first overcome by the presence of the promised Holy Spirit.

The Bible tells us that while the disciples were in a state of continuous prayer:

> ...a sound like the blowing of a violent wind came from heaven and filled the whole house where they were sitting. They saw what seemed to be tongues of fire that separated and came to rest on each of them. All of them were filled with the Holy Spirit and began to speak in other tongues as the Spirit enabled them.[8]

Many things can be gathered from this retelling of the event, and especially in its relationship to working with spirits. But, three aspects have always struck me as important.

1. The Spirit Must Arrive

First, the Holy Spirit specifically descends into the room and rests upon each person's head. This is reminiscent of Jesus' baptism by his cousin, John, when the Holy Spirit "descended on him in bodily form like a dove."[9] In both cases the Holy Spirit arrived from some other place. In neither case was the Holy Spirit already present. Not at the river. Not at the temple. Rather than being a pervasive energetic force, as it is often taught, the Holy Spirit descended from above.

One of the most explicit examples of the arrival of Spirit occurs further along in the Book of Acts:

> When the apostles in Jerusalem heard that Samaria had accepted the word of God, they sent Peter and John to Samaria. When they arrived, they prayed for the new believers there that they might receive the Holy Spirit, because **the Holy Spirit had not yet come on any of them**; they had simply been baptized in the name of the Lord Jesus. Then Peter and John placed their hands on them, and they received the Holy Spirit.[10] (emphasis mine)

Here we see that it wasn't until Peter and John placed their hands on a group of people who had already been in a state of great devotion that the Holy Spirit is said to have been "received" by them. Again, the Holy Spirit needed to be brought down, gifted, made to manifest in a place it was not.

Spirit work is a waiting game. It requires patience. Though many of us believe the spirit world to be separated from the human world by the thinnest of veils, it is still a threshold that must be crossed. In spirit work, this crossing of the threshold is initiated by a request made by the mediums in the room. Just as in the story of the Pentecost, when we sit with spirits, we invite, we coax, and, especially if it's getting late into the evening, we *demand* that the spirits enter our space. We typically do this through various means, be it song, prayer, silence, praise, and usually some combination of all of the above.

The passage above above is, in a way, even more telling. Despite the people mentioned having already been in a state of great devotion, and despite having been "baptised in the name of Lord Jesus," which, honestly, I would have assumed to be kind of a big deal for Christians, even they had not yet experienced the descent of the Spirit. So, while we could certainly say that spirit resides within the fabric of our world at all times, there is still a sense that the spirit of those who have passed, and certainly that most holy of spirits emanating directly from God through Jesus Christ, is prepared for by those who are actively trying to experience it. In effect, we must make space for spirit to arrive, because it is not necessarily already present with us.

Creating space for spirits is not just about lighting a few candles, saying a few words, and hoping for the best. On an interpersonal level—and I do believe that spirit work is enhanced by having great interpersonal skills—spirit work's "success" is in direct relation to how well we relate with the unseen world. In short, spirit work requires great communication skills. It requires great listening skills. It requires that you are reliable, that you do the things you say you're going to do to get in the spirit's good favor. It requires positivity and enthusiasm, knowing, without (too much) doubt or cynicism, that who you hope to come in contact with is both real and available to you. It requires nothing less than your highest form of relating. By being our best, most honest selves, we make room for spirits to come into our midst.

2. The Spirit Arrives Like a Glorious Noise

The second aspect of the story of Pentecost has to do with the manner in which the Holy Spirit descends into the room. In a number of instances we read about the Holy Spirit arriving for the first time as a cacophony. In Acts 2:2 we read about a "violent wind." In Acts 4:31 we're told that the place where the disciples were meeting was "shaken." In Mark 1:10 we read about "the heavens being torn apart." Each of these cases reminds us that the Holy Spirit's presence can be so contrary to mundane life as to be experienced as a complete rupture of this normality. The presence of the Holy Spirit disrupts the very fabric of existence, suggesting that the more tightly bound we are to our assumptions about the nature of reality, the greater we will feel the assault on these assumptions.

The Holy Spirit affects more than our surrounding environment. Despite the Holy Spirit being a spirit of peace, often symbolized by the image of a serene dove, the arrival of the Holy Spirit, and spirits in general, can be a disturbing affair to our bodies as well. Spirit work is body-centered, somatic work, which is especially apparent when we experience changes in ambient room temperature or on our skin. The image of a medium going into minor convulsions upon receiving a message from the spirit world is so widespread that it's become almost a cliché. And yet, no one who has had the experience of a spirit passing through the room can deny the tingling sensations that may run up and down a person's spine. Not to mention those caricatured shakes.

Each of these expressions of the presence of

spirits affect our bodies, our very own personal "spaces." So prevalent are these somatic expressions that entire religious movements have been named after them. Both the Religious Society of Friends and The United Society of Believers in Christ's Second Appearing, also known as the Quakers and the Shakers, two Christian sects founded in the 17th and 18th centuries respectively, were unceremoniously named after the bodily effects caused by the Holy Spirit.

3. The Spirit Wants Us to Speak

The third aspect of the story of Pentecost describes the ways in which the Holy Spirit commands people to speak aloud. Again, in Acts 2:4 it states that Jesus' followers "began to speak in other tongues as the Spirit enabled them." In Acts 4:31 it states, "And they were all filled with the Holy Spirit and spoke the word of God boldly." Later, in Acts 19:6, when Paul had begun his own mission, the Bible states, "When Paul placed his hands on [the people of Ephesus], the Holy Spirit came on them, and they spoke in tongues and prophesied." In the Gospel of Mark we learn that one of the signs of believers is the ability to "speak in new tongues."[11] Not to mention the prophets who were said to be inspired by the Spirit to write.[12]

Not only does spirit work depend on us communicating our experiences, but it also shows just how hard it is to resist doing so! The quickening of our human spirit seems to invoke a necessity to communicate. Anyone who has been truly inspired can attest to how powerful the urge is to share with others their experiences, and spirit work is no different.

So true is this need to communicate, that some forms of spirit work are based entirely on the transmitting of spirit messages in writing. Similar to the shamanic Bon practices of Tibet,[13] automatic writing, otherwise known as "spirit writing" or *psychography*, is a method in which a medium becomes a vehicle for spirits to write their messages down on paper. This is supposedly done without the medium's own conscious input into the messages being produced.

Gifts of the Spirit

Each of the above expressions of the Holy Spirit—it's descent into spaces, confrontation with those in waiting, and its influencing of people's communication—are signs confirming the presence of something non-ordinary within our midst. But, the Holy Spirit also bestows gifts, or "charisms," onto people. These charisms have a direct effect on our personal growth and the ways in which we interact in the material and spirit world. Paul seemed to have had intimate knowledge of these gifts of Spirit, and goes into detail about their natures:

There are different kinds of gifts, but the same Spirit distributes them…. [T]o each [person] the manifestation of the Spirit is given for the common good. To one there is given through the Spirit a message of wisdom, to another a message of knowledge by means of the same Spirit, to another faith by the same Spirit, to another gifts of healing by that one Spirit, to another miraculous powers, to another prophecy, to another distinguishing between spirits, to another speaking in different kinds of tongues, and to still another the interpretation of tongues. All these are the work of one and the same Spirit, and he distributes them to each one, just as he determines.[14]

Spirit workers are typically expected to work in service of the greater good, either by uplifting negative spirits, or by helping people in their community. One need look no further than to Paul's statement that "the Spirit is given for the common good" to see that even two thousand years ago people were warned against using the gifts of Spirit for boasting or self-aggrandizement. Instead, these gifts were to be employed for helping those in need and for healing those around us, each gift asking something different from us when it comes to how we offer it.

The Gift of Wisdom and Knowledge

> *He gave some measure of Wisdom to everyone,*
> *but poured her out on those who love him.*
> —Sirach 1:10

It is one thing to understand a teaching, to hear the words, and comprehend its meaning. It is another to know it to be true.

We know through experience. While we may understand that the snow we see through our window means that the temperature outside is below freezing, we *know* it is cold when we feel the tips of our noses burn from the chill. Knowledge is the embodiment of understanding. We know something is true when we feel it in our bones and guts.

Wisdom takes this further. Wisdom is the ability to build on what we know. Wisdom takes knowledge and creates something new. When this newness is spoken, it inspires others to do the same. Wisdom propels our knowning.

Traditionally, knowledge and wisdom are considered *of the spirit* then they are not dependent on understanding the content of the issue. The ability to speak eloquently on a subject one knows little about is a classic example. Inspired knowledge and wisdom speak as if on their own, from some other place. They are not reliant on our personal storehouses of acquired data.

When the Holy Spirit gifts us with knowledge and wisdom, we gain insight into problems we may know little about. Much of what comes up in group spirit work has to do with other peoples' health issues, interpersonal and relationship impasses, or confusions about which direction to take in creative or professional work. People often come to a spirit session hoping to solve a family matter, or wanting to fix a problem they're having at work or with a friend.

You may find that there is a particular clarity to what you say in regards to these matters while sitting with spirits, a fluidity in the order of words you are speaking that feels not entirely of your own doing. The nature of the information you impart is secondary to its source. You might find yourself discussing how to lean on the spirit world for assistance, while at the same time suggesting counseling or outside mediation services. For someone having trouble navigating difficult emotions you might relate specific examples given in relevant holy books for dealing with such matters, as well as options for therapeutic assistance.

The wisdom and knowledge you impart will relate to whatever is needed in the moment. The tone and flow of what's coming to you will give insight as to the source of the words.

The Gift of Faith

> *Now faith is confidence in what we hope for,*
> *and assurance about what we do not see.*
> —Hebrews 11:1

To have faith is to trust that something will behave or turn out the way you expect it to. We have faith that the train will arrive on time. We have faith that our good deeds will be well-received. Faith suggests a sense of stability. We feel secure having faith that a certain something will come to pass.

Faith in a spiritual context functions similarly to the above. We have faith that our spiritual practices will benefit us. We have faith that our religious traditions will support us during difficult times. We have faith in our spiritual teachers and guides, that they will give good council, and make themselves available as often as they can.

But, true faith hides within itself a subtle distance from the thing we expect to see come to fruition. Writer and professor of philosophy, John D. Caputo, writes, "faith is not safe. Faith is not faith all the way down, so that all the gaps and crevices of faith are filled with more faith and it all makes for a perfect, continuous and well-rounded whole."[15] According to Caputo, faith reads more like a woven piece of fabric rather than an indestructible steel rod. It's strength comes from the flexibility of its holey construction. In fact, one might say that faith, by definition, is based on holes in our knowing. As Caputo states, "faith is faith and not knowledge."[16] Faith exists in the space between ourselves and knowing, between ourselves and the outcome, which is always in a state of potential.

To live in this state of faith is to own our vulnerability. When two or more people decide to follow their feelings of love for one another and form a relationship together, each person places their faith between themselves and the other. In this space of vulnerability there is an energetic charge. Maybe even a magnetism.

The gift of faith is the gift of compassion. It's two people sitting in the seat of unknowing, hearts open, totally willing to engage with whatever comes up between them. In spirit work, or any other form of relating, there is no greater gift to give than a willingness to be present to whatever may come to pass.

The Gift of Healing

> *Is anyone among you sick? Let them call the elders of the church to pray over them and anoint them with oil in the name of the Lord. And the prayer offered in faith will make the sick person well; the Lord will raise them up. If they have sinned, they will be forgiven.*
>
> —James 5:14-15

The term "healer" has become so overused, and, in cases where there is little life experience to back it up, so baseless, that it can often feel meaningless. Everywhere you look in the spiritual corners of social media you will find healers willing to snip off what no longer serves you, smudge out what has thus far held you back, and detoxify what has been sickening you. With so many healers in the spiritual marketplace it's a wonder there is anyone left who needs healing!

A "healer" implies that someone has the extraordinary ability to fix another human being. But, from the perspective of the health practitioner, it is not the job of the therapist, clinician, or even the spirit worker to heal the client. Rather, it is our job to help create the conditions whereby the body-mind can heal itself *by the grace of God.*

When a doctor attempts to mend a broken bone, they disinfect the area of the breakage, set the bone back into place, and stabilize the region of the break with a cast. The actual healing process, the process whereby the bone "knits" itself back together, takes place in the patient's body on its own.

Spirit work is no different. To allow spirit to work through us is to allow spirit to help us create the conditions through which a person can heal themselves. This may come in the form of a comforting touch that soothes a person's anxiety, a message that breaks up a mental blockage, an herbal remedy that helps root out the cause or relieve the symptoms of an illness. In either case, spirit workers do not "fix" people. We assist people. And, it is through this assistance that we allow the miracle of healing to be fully expressed.

The Gift of Miraculous Powers

> Coming to his hometown, he began teaching the people in their synagogue, and they were amazed. "Where did this man get this wisdom and these miraculous powers?"
> —Matthew 13:54

The yogis of India have talked at great length about the various powers, or *siddhis*, that a person might obtain through rigorous spiritual practice. And yet, where siddhis are mentioned there often follows an admonition that powers, although having many benefits, usually cause harm to the spiritual pursuits of the practitioner. Patanjali, the great codifier of yogic philosophy, states in his Yoga Sutras that "[t]hese powers are accomplishments for the mind that is outgoing, but are obstacles to enlightenment."[17] In other words, though they are the natural products of spiritual effort, miraculous powers can easily become obstructions on the path.[18]

But, there is another way to look at how miraculous powers may function in a religious context. While it's true that within the Roman Catholic Church there has been a move to downplay miraculous abilities,[19] both the Charismatic and Pentecostal movements have embraced the gifts of the Holy Spirit in the form of healing abilities demonstrated through the laying on of hands and feats of dominion over nature through the practice of snake handling.

But, how does handling a poisonous snake benefit the common good?

Aside from the direct, physical effect a miracle might have on a person (curing blindness, disease, etc.), miracles have the ability to disrupt our appreciation of not only what we believe to be possible in the world, but also our understanding of the outer limits of what constitute "natural laws." In effect, miracles have the ability to open ourselves up to the power of God. They increase our awe, our *how can this possibly be-ness*, which in turn increases our reverence. This reverence folds us over. It humbles us. The world becomes a blessed unfamiliar. With unparalleled immediacy miracles increase our appreciation of just how vast this spiritual world really is, which inevitably renews our faith, itself a form of healing.

The Gift of Prophecy

No prophecy ever came from human initiative. Rather, when people spoke as messengers of

God, they did so under the inspiration of the Holy Spirit.
—2 Peter 1:21

Unlike the previously mentioned gifts, the function of prophecy comes across as a bit more straightforward. To prophesize is to make a statement about things that have yet to pass. In other words, to tell the future.

However, the word "prophecy" has a nuance to it that is sometimes missed. "Prophecy" comes from the Greek *propheteia*, which is defined as the "gift of interpreting the will of the gods." Therefore, prophecy, by definition, requires a relationship with God, since ultimately prophecy is not of oneself, but of God.

I like to think of prophecy as the ability to see down a long road stretched out in front of me. Ordinarily, conditions do not allow me to see very far. Maybe it's dark or foggy, making it difficult to see.

At some point, however, the sun begins to burn off the suspended moisture in the air, and the road in front of me becomes clear. If the sun has done its job well, I can see far off into the distance.

Prophecy is the ability to see the paths God has laid out in front of you. It's about following that path in your mind, and seeing what's coming up around a bend in the distance. Prophecy is insight into what's coming next. This gift becomes even more pronounced when we're able to offer it in service to other people.

The Gift of Having the Ability to Distinguish Between Spirits

> The Spirit clearly says that in later times some will abandon the faith and follow deceiving spirits and things taught by demons.
>
> —1 Timothy 4:1

As we will see later, the biblical worldview included a belief in the proliferation of spirits of varying qualities. We see this in Paul's letter to the Corinthians regarding the gifts of the Spirit, as well as through the words of the author of 1 Timothy.[20] From these two passages we can assume that "distinguishing between spirits" meant that the spirits could have both beneficial or detrimental qualities. Which is to say, if all spirits other than the Holy Spirit were malicious, distinguishing between them would not be necessary.

My own introduction to spirit work began when my teacher attempted to figure out who and of what nature were my accompanying spirits. During our first encounter Fernando tried to use speech. At other times he used divination. If ever he needed further confirmation, he consulted "the dead."[21]

Spirit work in the Afro-Caribbean tradition of

espiritismo, recognizes a number of distinct ethereal presences, known as the *comisiones*, many of whom show up during spiritual masses where they are encouraged to participate. These well-known spirits have been so consistent in their participation that their legacies and felt presences have lived on for decades, even hundreds of years. Many of the spirits have names, and are almost famous within the spirit worker world, appearing at any number of circles around the globe.

For the initiated, discerning who of the comisiones is present in a spiritual mass can be a relatively simple task, as these spirits are often easily recognized by their distinct individual behaviors and mannerisms. However, spirits who exist outside this cadre of beings can be harder to pin down.

Fernando wanting my spirit to speak was his way of discerning the disposition of my spirit. Was it beneficial, malicious, misleading, or ultimately harmless? While much of this discernment is subjective (i.e. a spirit that simply has nice things to say about people, might be considered beneficial, if of little consequence) the ability to distinguish between spirits is ultimately an artform. Perfecting this art allows us to help people exponentially increase their knowledge of who and what is helping or harming them as they walk their life's path.

The Gift of Speaking in Tongues and Interpreting Tongues

> For anyone who speaks in a tongue does not speak to people but to God. Indeed, no one understands them; they utter mysteries by the Spirit.
> —1 Corinthians 14:2

"Glossolalia" can be defined as the trance-induced speech of someone having a religious experience. What some people call "speaking in tongues." What others call "nonsense."

Mirriam-Webster defines language, correctly in my opinion, as "audible, articulate, meaningful sound as produced by the action of the vocal organs." By this definition, glossolalia is a language. Though, this may not be immediately apparent.

While no one can deny that the act of speaking in tongues is both audible and produced by the vocal organs, one might find difficulty accepting that it is either articulate or meaningful. In reality, it is both.

Meaning is subjective; assigned and agreed upon within communities. It is determined by a thing's use value *in the moment*, and remains forever in flux *between moments*. Poetry is meaningful when it moves us, or changes the way we experience the world. It is meaningless when it doesn't resonate. Speaking in tongues is meaningful because it dramatically shifts the experience of those witnessing it. The "words" themselves may not be definable, but they do have meaning. In the moment, they affect us.

Still, one could ask, is it articulate? A person having trouble articulating is still using language. They might be having difficulty getting their point across, but we'd never assume that they weren't speaking. Glossolalia is not only a form of speaking, it is a form of articulated speech. Never have I witnessed a person speaking in tongues become frustrated with getting their message across. In fact, they often appear to fully comprehend what they are saying, often enjoying the fact that some people seem stupefied. It is the people in attendance who must do the work to understand. The medium is articulating just fine. It's the job of those in attendance to grasp what's being spoken.

The language of spirits, in its anarchic assault on conventional speech, disrupts normative modes of communication. Its internal logic changes case-by-case. It is maximalist, even avant-garde speech, expressed in whatever capacity the human vessel conveying it can physically handle. It is sound poetry removed from the art gallery, and injected into the basement labs of mystic scientists.

Because of its non-conforming nature, it is easy to see why Paul considered not only the ability to speak in tongues a gift of the Holy Spirit, but also the ability to understand what is being said as equally a holy gift. Glossolalia needs to be interpreted if the message is to be made relevant. The interpretation is what makes speaking in tongues a true language. Interpretation begets conversation, therefor the interpreter emboldens the language, giving it power and a reason to be.

The Holy Spirit Guides Us Toward Community

The above gifts show just how personal our relationships are with the Divine. Though the gifts come from a single source, the singularity cleaves into a myriad of expressions, each piece uniquely fitting to our personality.

And yet, Paul warns against separating ourselves from one another, speaking of our efforts being a gift not only for ourselves, but also for the common good. In our individualist society we often think that we need to do everything on our own; that we shouldn't need help from anyone. Even the DIY punk ethos I grew up with, which spoke of a revolutionary self-reliance and independence from mainstream social conventions, still hid an underlying individualism that many of us tempered with communitarianism and mutual aid.

The Holy Spirit is also described in individualistic terms. Unique gifts are given to specific people. Each person has a special relationship with the Divine. On the surface this may infer that Christian spirituality is meant to be a solitary affair. And yet, Paul's suggestion that no one person will possess all of what the Holy Spirit has to offer speaks to something more communal. Instead of taking our spiritual gifts and running away to live in a cave, we are asked to live in community with others who will inevitably possess qualities we ourselves may not have.

By recognizing and accepting that we will only possess some of what the Holy Spirit has to offer, we place ourselves among those who possess the qualities and talents that each of us require. In doing so, we find that we can look to others for the wisdom and knowledge we may need, for the faith we may need, for the healing we may need. We can come into communion with those who display extraordinary abilities, vision, and foresight. We can keep close to us people who might help distinguish between what does and what does not serve us. We can look to those who have the ability to interpret a sometimes confusing and unintelligible landscape for guidance.

In these ways we may come together to honor and give expression both to the spirits among us, as well as the gifts given to us through the one Holy Spirit. With this we pray:

> "May I use my gifts well, Spirit of God, and may I respect the gifts of others."[22]

Chapter 4
Not-So-Holy Spirits

A spirit glided past my face, and the hair on my body stood on end.
—Job 4:15

ALL SOCIETIES have ways in which they incorporate the elements of life that hide in the periphery, the so-called "dark" elements of life. Even our largely materialist culture has retained some of the ritualistic aspects of death and the unknown. We still go to funerals, most cemeteries are open to the public, and Halloween remains one of the most anticipated holidays of the year. One could argue that watching thrillers on television, playing violent video games, and going to see gruesome horror films are all ways in which we ritualize the macabre aspects of our human experiences.

Were spirit work to involve only the most beneficent of forces, beings of light flickering about with only the best of intentions, it's likely that this work would have faded into the background further and faster than it already has. We humans are fascinated by darkness, and any opportunity to explore what we don't know tickles our interest to no end. Having evolved into upright, forward-seeing bipeds, biologically determined to see more or less only what is in front of our faces, has made all things existing outside our periphery both tantalizing and potentially dangerous. So, it is not surprising that spirit work, and its dealings with unseen things, has been plagued by controversy and bolstered by intrigue.

And yet, while far too much has been made of the darker aspects of spirit work, a spiritual practice that deals primarily in the currency of light, it would be disingenuous to forgo a discussion of what lurks in the shadows.

Casting Out "Demons"

When it comes to discussions of "the spirits," the Christian tradition gives primacy to the Holy Spirit. As we have seen in the previous chapter, according to the apostle Paul, the presence of the Holy Spirit in a person's life is considered foundational if that life is to be considered truly inspired. However, the Holy Spirit, albeit central to our spiritual growth, is still one spirit among many. And, based on the number of references to banishing we find in the Bible, it would appear the earliest followers of Jesus agreed.

There are a number of stories in the Bible depicting what translators have described as Jesus casting out demons. In the Gospel of Matthew we read about one of the most well known:

> When he arrived at the other side in the re-
> gion of the Gadarenes, two demon-possessed
> men coming from the tombs met him. They
> were so violent that no one could pass that
> way. 'What do you want with us, Son of God?'
> they shouted. 'Have you come here to torture
> us before the appointed time?' Some distance
> from them a large herd of pigs was feed-
> ing. The demons begged Jesus, 'If you drive
> us out, send us into the herd of pigs.' Jesus
> said to them, 'Go!' So they came out and
> went into the pigs, and the whole herd rushed
> down the steep bank into the lake and died in
> the water.[23]

In the Gospel of Luke we read of a similar oc-
currence where Jesus rebukes a demon who has
taken control over a man's body. Just as the demon was demanding that Jesus leave its presence,
Jesus commands the demon to "Be quiet!" and
come out of the possessed man. At which point
"the demon threw the man down before them all,
and came out without injuring him."[24]

These well known stories of Jesus casting out
"demons," the word itself based on a translation of
the Greek word *daimon*, have for centuries rein-
forced the theological argument in favor of both
exorcisms and spirit work.[25] In the Bible, Jesus not
only commands his followers to love as he loved,

preach as he preached, baptise as he baptised, but also states that among the many signs of the most devout of his followers will be their ability to speak in new tongues, pick up snakes without being bitten, safely drink poison, heal the sick, and, for the purposes of this chapter, drive out demons.[26] This is the biblical basis for the many dramatic images of church-going snake handlers and those who practice laying on of hands.

While all communities, religious or otherwise, are guilty of some form of "othering," it is because of Christianity's unique place as having been the de facto religion of a number of the world's empires, that it has had a particularly strong, and at many times, inhumane effect on the world's population, much of which has been based on its admonition of the Other as demonic.

Today, the word "demon" is a fiercely loaded term, synonymous with the "devil," and has for millenia been used to malign, discredit, and oppress people outside Christianity's arbitrary borders. Everything from certain styles of music, sexual orientations, mental health issues, other religious traditions, and political ideologies have at one time or another been deemed "demonic."

This insidious othering has had devasting effects. The various witch trials throughout Europe during the fifteenth and eighteenth centuries resulted in the execution of at least fifty thousand people, most of whom were women, many of whom were burned alive at the stake. In the newly forming colonies in America twenty people were executed, all but four being women, and all but one, who was crushed to death by stones, were hanged.

The Satanic Panic of the 1980s had parents falsely accusing Heavy Metal bands of hiding satanic messages in their records. Messages that were supposedly revealed only by playing the albums backwards. Not to mention the allegations of satanic ritual abuses in child daycare centers that were later debunked.

Much of this panic came to a head in the early nineties when Damien Echols, Jessie Misskelley, Jr., and Jason Baldwin, otherwise known as The Memphis Three, were wrongly convicted of murdering three young boys in Arkansas as part of a satanic ritual. Echols was sentenced to death. Misskelley and Baldwin were given life sentences. All three were eventually acquitted and released from prison in 2011, and since then Echols has gone on to become a writer, lecturer, and teacher of occult studies.

THERE HAS ALWAYS BEEN A PROBLEM using Jesus' casting out of demons as a theological justification for demonizing the Other. In the original Greek, the word "daimon" does not correspond to what we today would call a "demon," and especially not with the heavy emotional load that comes with it.

In modern English the connotations of the word "demon" refer more to the Greek word, *diabolo*, or "devil" as it appears in 1 Peter 5:8, "Your enemy, the devil (diabolos), prowls around like a roaring lion looking for someone to devour," or in James 4:7 "Submit yourselves, then, to God. Resist the devil (diabolo), and he will flee from you." Earlier, when Jesus is driven into the wilderness by the Spirit (Pneuma), he is tempted by this same "diabolou."

By contrast, a daimon in the Ancient Greek was more akin to the lingering spirits of people who had died, nature spirits, and various unseen forces. In his book, *Greek Religion*, German scholar of Greek mythology, Walter Burkert, takes this idea further into the ephemeral, stating that the term daimon "does not designate a specific class of divine beings, but a peculiar mode of action." Daimons are "a force that drives man forward where no agent can be named."[27] Referring to that which remains after a person dies, Burkert looks to Plato who felt that "all who die fighting for their country should be honored as a daemones." This idea was so universally accepted during the Hellenistic era—the time period leading up to the birth of Jesus—that it became common practice to refer to any person who had died as a daimon on their gravestone.[28]

The idea that after death the daimons of those who died would become intermediaries between humanity and the divine is found again in the writings of Plato. In *Symposium*, Plato describes daimons as "entities who stand in the middle between gods and men," and "communicate the messages and gifts from men to gods and gods to men."[29] Compare this to any description of what occurs in a typical séance, and we can see that the belief that the dead communicate with the living has had a long history.

In contrast, the idea that daimons were overwhelmingly malicious in disposition comes from Plato's student, Xenocrates, who believed that "it is [the daimons] who bring about diseases, barrenness of the earth, and discord among citizens."[30] This sentiment became so prevalent that we see it echoed almost six hundred years later in the third century bishop, St Cyprian. In his treatise, "On the Vanity of Idols," he refers to daimons as "impure and wandering spirits, who, after having been steeped in earthly vices, have departed from their celestial vigour by the contagion of earth, and do not cease, when [having already] ruined themselves, to seek the ruin of others."[31] To St Cyprian the daimons were inherently mischievous and miserable, determined to turn the living in kind. In effect, daimons were the (dis)embodiment of the phrase "misery loves company."

And yet, despite St Cyprian's negative stance toward daimons, what's significant is that he calls them spirits. He does not call them demons. Instead, they are the remaining subtle matter of human beings long past.

Returning to Matthew we can now see that it is not demons who were to be sent into the swine, but the spirits of dead people who happened to be of a particularly malicious disposition.[32] Even Mark 16:17 mentioned above, which lists "driving out demons" as a sign of those who have become devout followers of Christ, refers not to diabolos, or devils, but to *daimonia* or, as we might call them, the lingering spirits of humans with ill intent.

The earliest of the four gospels is further evidence of a world inhabited by malicious human spirits. Contrasting Matthew's account of the man from Gerasenes with Mark's earlier account of the same story proves such a point. In Mark's version, the Greek word "daimon" is not found. Rather, Mark refers to what speaks through the man as a "pneumati," which directly translates as "spirit," and is the same word used in the New Testament when mentioning the *Pneumati Hagio*, or Holy Spirit. In this similar section of the story, Mark states, "[The spirit] shouted at the top of his voice, 'What do you want with me, Jesus, Son of the Most High God? In God's name don't torture me!' For Jesus had said to him, 'Come out of this man, you impure spirit!'"[33]

Most scholars believe that Mark was penned before the three other Gospels, being the textual basis off which both Matthew and Luke were written.[34] This proves that in the earliest days of Jesus' ministry, and certainly by the earliest accounts as told by Mark, lingering spirits were believed to be numerous, of potentially malicious intent, and able to both enter, as well as be cast out of people.

The Evil Spirits That Block Your Liberation

The distinction between spirit and demon is an important one to be made. The modern emphasis on demons, with all the negative connotations the word carries, has led to a combative approach to working with the tormented residues of past lives, or what we might today call generational trauma.[35]

From a psychological perspective our daimons become aspects of ourselves to explore. Existentialist psychologist, Rollo May, echoes this sentiment in his book, *Love and Will*, where he describes the daimonic as "*any natural function which has the power to take over the whole person.* Sex and eros, anger and rage, and the craving for power are examples. The daimonic can be either creative or destructive and is normally both."[36] To May, the daimonic functions as a force within us. When these forces are allowed to pass through us as passing states, we remain in a state of relative peace and balance. If, however, we are overcome by the daimonic, we become, in a way, "possessed." As May states, "When this power goes awry, and one element usurps control over the total personality, we have 'daimon possession,' the traditional name through history for psychosis."[37]

Unless we engage with the daimonic, we will not be able to experience the beauty of life's myriad of emotional experiences. As May states, "In the daimonic lies our vitality, our capacity to open ourselves to the power of eros."[38] In other words, by entering into the daimonic or spirit realm, we are able to engage with what motivates us.

If we want to experience life in its fullest expression, avoiding "daimonic possession" does not seem to be an option. In *Symbols of Transformation* Carl Jung discusses the vitality of the daimonic as being propulsive and motivational, pushing us into new emotional and psychological spaces. However, this is not without discomfort. When this vitality bumps up against our rigid belief systems, the experience can be jarring. As a retaliation against our impulse to reject challenges to our beliefs, what Jung calls our "barriers against the dark," Jung states that "[t]he daemon throws us down, makes us traitors to our ideals and cherished convictions—traitors to the selves we thought we were."[39] In effect, the daimon functions, in part, as a way of forcing us to see in ourselves what we may not want to see.

Learning to see the unseen is reflected in the Gospel of John where we read about a blind man who was healed by Jesus. As the story goes, after a short discourse where Jesus tells his disciples that no, it was not sin that caused the man to be blind, but rather to show how God's work manifests in the world, Jesus states:

> "While I am in the world, I am the light of the world." He then spit on the ground, made some mud with the saliva, and put it on the blind man's eyes. 'Go,' he told him, "wash in the Pool of Siloam." So the man went and washed, and came home seeing.[40]

Another, shorter, example occurs in the Gospel of Luke where Jesus is described as "driving out a malicious force that was mute. When the force left, the man who had been mute spoke, and the crowd was amazed."[41]

These two examples show how unexamined aspects of our psyche have the ability to blind us to what goes on around us, as well as censor our ability to speak. The ways in which we close ourselves or have been closed off by others—our resistance to change, the censoring of our voices, our not wanting to see into our shadows—can all lead to a deadening of our spirit, a muting of the expressions of our vitality, a blinding to what will ultimately grow us.

Going Toward the Shadow

The longevity of a story's influence comes not from the particulars of the narrative, but from its ability to speak beyond itself. In literalist circles bent on making a celebrity out of Jesus, these stories serve only to demonstrate the awesome power of Jesus' miraculous abilities. After all, who else can do such amazing things?! For literalists, it's enough to prove how great Jesus was.

But, there are other ways to engage with these narratives, ways that take us far deeper into ourselves.

While it is certainly fascinating to think that Jesus was able to use a plaster of mud created from his saliva to give sight to a blind man (and who of us doesn't want to know the secrets to *that* recipe?!), what I find most inspiring is that Jesus, the great spirit worker who "commands even the unclean spirits,"[42] liberates the potential of the people he encounters by bringing their obstructions into the light. Jesus does not run from the spirit. He deliberately moves toward it.

This "going toward" is a reminder that liberation often comes through direct engagement with what imprisons us. We do not combat oppressive social structures by turning away from them. We confront them. We shine light on the injustice.

We see this in other cultural narratives as well. In *Feeding Your Demons*, Buddhist teacher, Lama Tsultrim Allione, quotes the twelfth century *tantrika*, Machig Labdron, who advises those of us on the spiritual quest to "tenderly" surround ourselves "with the hostile gods and demons of apparent existence."[43] Like Jesus, for Labdron the "demons" are not entities to run from, but are aspects of ourselves that we must engage with if we wish to know both their origin and their means of release. To Labdron, a demon is anything that hinders liberation.[44] In other words, a malicious spirit can function as a spiritual blockage, an aspect of ourselves we have yet to unpack.

Compare this to Mark 2:17 where Jesus states that "it is not the healthy who need a doctor, but the sick. I have not come to call the righteous, but sinners." Here, Jesus reminds us that these seemingly negative aspects of ourselves and of our environment are to be directly engaged with. Our perceived limitations, blind spots, and shadows, what in the past might have been called "evil entities," are not to be avoided, but to be explored. And, who better to bring to light what hides in our shadows than those who live there?

Lingering Spirits Don't Go to Therapy

Since so much of what comes up in spirit work has to do with personal problems or relational impasses, when talking about spirit work from the perspective of self-growth, it's important to recognize when negative spirits behave as a mirror for self-reflection, or as a spotlight that can illuminate aspects of ourselves hiding out in the shadows.

And yet, from the perspective of traditional

spirit work, there are times when more than our personal shadow self is what's causing the problem. Sometimes, the awful feelings in a person's home are caused, not by the internalized condemnations of one's father, but by a disembodied spirit that has crossed the threshold separating the living and the dead.

Famed spiritist, Allan Kardec, believed in, and spoke with, this breed of spirits. He believed the spirits of humans lingered long after the human host died, and, in certain circumstances, and under the right conditions, communicated with the living.

He also believed that spirits differed in their characters and personalities. In his seminal text, *The Spirits' Book*, Kardec, relays the teachings he received through a number of mediums on the nature of the varying qualities of the spirits a person might encounter.[45] For example, when asked the question "Are all spirits equal or is there some kind of hierarchy among them?" Kardec is told by the spirits that they "are of different orders, according to their individual degree of self-purification." As the spirits described it:

> In the first order we may put those who have already reached perfection: the pure spirits. In the second are those who have reached the middle of the scale: their main concern is the desire to do the good. In the third are those

who are toward the bottom of the scale: the imperfect Spirits. These are characterized by ignorance, the desire for evil and all the passions that delay their advancement.[46]

When asked by Kardec "Are all the spirits of the third order altogether evil?" the spirits respond:

No, some do neither good nor evil; others, however, take pleasure in evil and are satisfied when they find an opportunity for it. Still others are frivolous or *foolish* spirits, more mischievous than evil, and they also take pleasure in amusing themselves by bewildering people and causing them petty annoyances.[47]

Kardec expands on the information given to him by the spirits, writing that "impure spirits" are prone to giving "unscrupulous advice" and inciting "discord and distrust," their motivations being the same as when they were incarnated as humans.[48] During their life on earth "they do evil for the pure pleasure of it, most often without reason."[49]

Kardec recognized that spirits often reenact their lived behavior patterns in the afterlife. Like St Cyprian, Kardec believed that if you were an annoyance while living, there's a good chance you will be the same postmortem.

Kardec goes on to discuss what he calls "Boisterous and Disturbing Spirits," which correspond to those who "make their presence known through perceptible and physical effects, such as raps, the movement and abnormal displacement of solid objects, the movement of air, etc." Curiously, this class of spirits are "more attached to matter than the others."[50] In many ways this class of spirits replicate the behavior of ghosts or poltergeists.

Regardless of what level or class a malicious spirit can be identified as, when such a being decides to enter and disrupt our personal space, the question that comes to mind is "Why?" Why go about the post-corporeal life in the same manner as one did in the corporeal state? If living a life of bitterness toward those around you didn't fill the void we all recognize is a part of the human condition, why not try a new approach? Why must those spirits who on earth ruined their own lives, continue to "seek the ruin of others" in the afterlife?

There is something to be said about cycles of hurt and the perpetuation of emotional neglect among people who were not properly loved as children. How many emotionally distant people have you come across who themselves come from households that were less than nurturing? If we are to believe that the varying personalities wandering through the afterlife behave the way they do because of their previous experiences on Earth, then we must accept that their behavior is a continuation of this cycle of trauma. So-called "bad spirits" can be nothing more than the negative energetic remnants of people who lived before us. They are someone's ancestors, still working through their "stuff."

St Cyprian was not a modern psychologist, and certainly not a Marxist one. He spoke of less-than-pleasant spirits as the residual matter of people who "ruined themselves" after having lived a life "steeped in earthly vices." He did not speak about these same people as having been ruined by a society that was incapable of caring for its citizens. He did not speak of them as victims of a greater uncompassionate evil. Similarly, Kardec spoke of spirits that disturbed the peace as the lingering aspects of people who once lived a life of evil "for the pure pleasure of it," and "most often without reason."

Neither he nor St Cyprian recognized that these people did not live in a vacuum. While we are all responsible for the ways we express our trauma, no one behaves aggressively "without reason." Like the people among us who are living, and who may not behave in ways we find amiable, so-called malicious spirits are stuck in a traumatic feedback look. They deserve our compassion, even if we may need to set up healthy boundaries between us and them in order to protect ourselves.

In his book, *Mesa Blanca*, spirit medium, Florencio Guevara, discusses how one might go about dealing with negative spirits who have yet to process their lived experiences. His approach requires the spirit to own its negative influence, and take responsibility for its behavior. Guevara states that the governing medium of the *misa*, or séance, should "instruct the entity to lift all the negativity it has wrought on the subject," as well as "plead forgiveness." The "interrogator," as Guevara calls the medium, should speak directly, almost personally, to the "dark spirit":

> Follow the instructions of those spirits of light. They will be leading you to a much better place where you will find peace for your soul and be able to grow. Someday you will be in the light and free.
>
> Then you will be returning to perform as a positive force and undo all the accumulated damage you have done to others as well as yourself. Now leave the medium without disturbing the quadrant! In the name of God, bless you and safe passage![51]

For Guevara, spirits that bring negativity are to be worked with. They are not to be maligned. One of the functions of the spirit medium is to uplift those spirits who may be lingering on the material plane due to unprocessed events in their life. As a practitioner of espiritismo, which was heavily influenced by the spiritist teachings of Allan Kardec, his idea that spirits remain or linger in order to work out unfinished business lines up nicely with Kardec's teachings. For Guevara, it is the job of those with the spiritual skills to both rid people of negative spiritual influence, as well as help elevate spirits to their highest potential.

Embrace the Shadows

> *Perhaps everything terrible is in its deepest being something helpless that wants help from us.*
> —Rainer Maria Rilke

Negativity is difficult to be around. Ideas and expressions that are unfamiliar can be off-putting or frightening. Not-knowing often makes us feel insecure.

Throughout the centuries people have found different ways of dealing with these sometimes less-than-pleasurable experiences. In cases where people felt assaulted by the unknown, where the darkness was seen as an aberration to all that was good in the world, people lashed out, sometimes physically retaliating against what they believed to be the source of their uncomfortable feelings. Others, who recognized that darkness exists in us all, attempted to work with what appeared to be frightening.

Between Jesus' direct engagement with what obstructed people's human potential; St Cyprian's disdain for dark forces he felt were intent on destroying humanity; the psychological philosophies of May and Jung, which tended to see dark forces not as external entities, but as aspects of ourselves; and Florencio Guevara who sees the role of the medium as beneficial to those spirits suffering in the liminal state; between all of these exists a common bond of exploration.

No matter the stance one takes, what lurks in the shadows is to be seen. Whether to be expunged from a person's life, or embraced as a guidepost along the spiritual path, what hides out in our periphery has an effect on our lives. It is our job to understand the details of that effect as much as humanly possible. And, as someone who sits with spirits, you are in one of the best positions to do exactly that.

Chapter 5
Spirit and the Self

SPIRITUAL BYPASS is the act of using spirituality to ignore unresolved negative psychological and emotional patterns in oneself.[52] Social media, having become the primary platform through which many people perform their spirituality—often in their homes, far from real-time interactions with people, and without checks on their behavior—has made spiritual bypass a considerable issue within online spiritual communities.

So, before moving into the practices one might do to become sensitive to the realm of spirits, we will first look at who it is that does the doing, with an eye toward disrupting this pervasive trend.

What the Hell Am I?

What is your life? You are a mist that appears for a little while and then vanishes.
—James 4:14

Personally, I think James is letting us off easy.

When I look around, I see more than a few examples of human intervention that suggest we are a bit more than "a mist." Wars are not started at the whims of mist. Inequality is not the result of mists vying for power. Mists do not prioritize profits over people.

So, while I agree that the relatively short life of a human can pass as if fleeting, the havoc one can cause in the interim reminds me just how important the interval is between life and death. It is this interval which I am concerned with, and which has led me to the conclusion that our humanness consists not only of a misty effervescence, but of three very distinct aspects: consciousness, spirit, and self.

Our consciousness, sometimes called our awareness, other times called the witness of our experiences, is found deep within us. It is the quiet center, accessed through silent meditation, where we are able to sit and observe our thoughts and emotions, as they arise, with a pleasant sense of detachment. If there is such a thing as a happy place within us, then consciousness would be that place.

Our spirit is what moves and motivates us. It can be quickened, depleted, or at rest depending on any number of factors, including our outlook on life, our health, and the information we take in from the outside world. Our spirit is often expressed through our drives.

Our self is the curated version of who we think we are projected out into the world. It is also a filter that sifts what we take in through our senses. Our self is a protection mechanism. It helps us navigate the world.

With regards to spirit work, one might think that "spirit" would be the aspect we would be most interested in. After all, it's the aspect of ourselves that has the potential to linger after we die.

And yet, it isn't spirit which usually needs our attention. Spirit is a matter of fact. It is our birthright. "God formed a human from the dust of the ground and breathed into its nostrils the breath of life, and the human being became a living being."[53] In other words, spirit is what animates us. The self, on the other hand, is what tempers this animation. And, it is therefore the self which most often needs to be assessed when navigating the world of spirit and spirit communication.

The Self at Play in the World

Think of a time when you were feeling overjoyed and full of spirit, but had to reign in the expression of your happiness due to the company you were in. Perhaps you were at a funeral where going around telling people how psyched you were to be alive would have been frowned upon. Although positivity and affirmations are said to "quicken" our spirit, there are times when expressing such experiences is considered inappropriate, if not insensitive. In these instances our self tempers the quickened spirit in an effort to make us behave more appropriately given the circumstances.

Now, think of a time when you were feeling down. Perhaps you had just received some bad news, but, because of the situation you were in, had to put on a "happy face." In this case the self rummaged through its closet of costumes, the "kinds" of you it had stored away, and found a version of your personality that suited the situation. In this way the self projected a "happy you" to mask the state of your dampened spirit.

In both of these instances your self calibrated the expression of your spirit in order to conform to what was expected of you in the world. Were the self not to be there, your spirit would, for better or worse, soar and nosedive, ungoverned for all the world to see, at all times. The self makes sure this doesn't happen too often.

But, the self has another function. Not only does the self filter what we project outward, but it also filters how we take in and perceive the world around us. The self wants to protect us, and it attempts to do so by shielding us from experiences in the world that might damage our well-designed sense of who we think we are.

Over the course of our life we collect what, in the yogic tradition, are called *samskaras*, or imprints.[54] Today we might call these triggers. They're the aspects of an experience that we hold onto, usually unconsciously, either for protection (i.e. you were bit by a dog as a child, so now you are afraid of all dogs), or for affirmation (i.e. people like when you wear red, so you decide to wear red more often). This is all totally normal for us humans, and is part of how we survive in the world. We remember to avoid what we consider to be dangerous in order to avoid harm. We increase our security by projecting a personality into the world that is attractive to others so they stay close, in the hopes that they will help keep us safe.

Problems arise, however, when we let our samskaras inform every decision we make. If I was bit by a dog as a child, and, as a protection mechanism, refused to be friends with anyone who had a dog, my world would quickly begin to shrink. If I decided to throw out every piece of clothing I owned that wasn't red, I'd find myself doing laundry every other day to make up for the deficit in clean clothes.

Over time, the accumulation of samskaras limits our potential. But, rather than work on the limits our samskaras have placed on us so as to gain more freedom in the world, many of us work overtime to create new conditions that conform to our samskaras. In other words, we create a new reality outside to match what we experience inside. If red is the only color I'm willing to wear, because it's the only color I think people will like seeing me in, rather than challenge my beliefs about acceptance, I reinforce opportunities to shop at online stores that only sell red clothing.

If this were only about wearing red all the time, there'd be little pause for concern. But, from a yogic perspective, we're creating new samskaras on a daily basis, binding ourselves to thousands of new triggers year after year. Because of this we find ourselves having to constantly refashion exteriors that conform in more and more nuanced ways to our internal experiences. And, this takes effort.

With this in mind, let's go back to our original exercise. Think of a time when you may have overreacted to a situation. Let's imagine that regardless of how justified you felt in the moment, eventually you came to believe that your response was disproportionate to the circumstances. We often call this "reactivity." But, what causes us to be so reactive?

Reactivity occurs when one of our samskaras gets bumped, setting off an alarm inside of us. Our heart starts racing. We might begin to sweat or feel tightness in our muscles. At this point, our thinking mind goes into panic mode attempting to find ways to shut off the siren, and reduce the physical sensations.

While we might think that this happens only in extreme circumstances relating to overtly traumatizing experiences in our past (i.e. abuse, witnessing a death, being a victim of a violent crime), the truth is we are in protection mode all the time. You do not need to have experienced a violent trauma to create samskaras. Many of our samskaras impressed themselves upon us in small ways during our childhood, when we had few opportunities and skills to express our feelings and emotions. This is how a rejection from your high school crush on a day you forgot to wear deodorant might cause you, thirty years later, to lash out at the cashier whenever your local market is out of your favorite soap.

Being in protection mode all the time causes stress, and our thinking mind, the mind where our thoughts are racing non-stop, is constantly trying to figure out how to settle our nerves, usually in ways that don't ultimately serve us. Nevertheless, we attach our attention to these thoughts whenever one seems to have come up with a solution to the problem. This attachment to the incessant chatter of the mind is called "the monkey mind," and it is from this place where much of the confusion arises in our spiritual practice.

Internalized voices

> Just as a monkey swinging through the trees grabs one branch and lets it go to seize another, so too, that which is called thought, mind, or consciousness arises and disappears continually both day and night.
> —Siddhartha Gautama, The Buddha

It can be difficult to speak authentically, or trust the communication we receive from Spirit. Many of the issues that arise when practicing spirit work have to do with getting out of our own way.

Known in Buddhism as *kapacitta*, the monkey-mind relates to the constant agitated restlessness of our internal monologue, the contents of which make up the estimated 70,000 thoughts we have per day. We may choose to ignore how these thoughts might differ from one another, but not all voices within our head have the same source

Over the course of our lives we internalize the thoughts and opinions of other people and of the society at large. And, from this internalization we speak ourselves into the world. Jesus says as much in the Gospel of Matthew where he states, "A good person produces good things from the treasury of a good heart, and an evil person produces evil things from the treasury of an evil heart."[55] Jesus affirms the idea that we internalize our experiences of the world around us, the effects of which he distinguishes as being either "good" or "evil." The term "evil" may catch some off guard, but it is an interesting usage. "Evil" comes from the Greek *poneros*, which carries connotations of annoyances, harassing labors, and hardship. And, is not carrying negative thoughts, at the very least, an annoying, burdensome, hardship?[56]

Jesus believed the heart held multitudes. He did not believe it to be solely a vessel of love and compassion. For Jesus, the heart was neutral, and spoke on behalf of its owner. "[O]ut of the abundance of the heart the mouth speaks."[57] How compassionate we must be with ourselves, with these overburdened hearts brimming with negativity.

We see this in our speech. How many *I'm so stupid*'s and *I look awful today*'s have you caught yourself expressing? These acidic thoughts were taught to us, and we express them even though, inherently, we know this language is abusive. Can you imagine saying such things to a friend, telling someone you care about that they look awful? And yet, most of us have expressed these thoughts to ourselves thousands of times. But, whose voice is it that criticizes us so harshly?

Whose voice is telling you that "no one is going to talk to you at the party?" Whose voice is harshly judging your friends for being five minutes late? The source of many of these voices is pre-verbal, woven into the fabric of our psychological makeup as children before we even had a voice. These are learned voices.

This is the mental landscape many of us exist in when we begin walking the spiritual path. Spiritual practice often consists of methods which help us find ways to subvert our attachments to this mental chatter. Unfortunately, many people have not had the opportunity to do such work, and find themselves coming to practices like spirit work without having first unpacked the baggage of their mind. Imagine all that chatter going on as you open yourself up to another set of voices from the spirit realm. Can you imagine how confusing that might be? Caught inside our internal commentary, how do we know which voice to listen to? How do we know which voice to *not* listen to? How do we know which voice should speak when communicating spirit to other people?

Projection and Transference

A good spirit worker must be able to observe the manifestation of their thoughts rather than be led aimlessly by them. In short, someone who wishes to engage with spirits needs to be able to ignore the distractions of the 70,000 daily thoughts *at will*.

Spirit workers who have not done the work of releasing their attachments to the fluctuations of the mind, risk burdening people with their own unprocessed baggage. They risk falling into spiritual bypass, which usually leads to some form of projection and transference.

The term "projection" refers to the act of "projecting" our feeling state on someone who is not necessarily feeling the same as we do. When we accuse someone of being angry at us, when in fact it is we who are angry at them, that is projection. When we're offering communication from the spirit world to another person, informing them that we are being told that they are behaving dishonestly, when in fact we are the ones who are being dishonest, this is projection.

Transference takes it one step further. Transference happens when we "transfer" what we have learned about our behaviors in the past onto people in the present, altering our behaviors to prepare for that response. For example, we exhibit transference when we refuse to express ourselves in public, because we assume people will make fun of you, based on previous experiences. This may show up while communicating spirit to another person when we censor what we're receiving, because we assume the other person is going to get mad. Not because the person is necessarily prone to anger. But, because people in our past have been angered by things we have said.

NOW, PERHAPS YOU'RE WONDERING, *What does all of this have to do with engaging the spirit world*?

People who consider themselves to be spiritual teachers and guides are just as guilty of projecting their feelings and transferring their childhood grievances onto their clients and students as anyone else. This often comes in the form of unsolicited spiritual guidance and overzealous "you need to know this right now" proclamations.

Recognizing when we're projecting or displaying transference is absolutely necessary, if we intend to share our spirit communications with others. Learning to tease out the quality of the voices in our head, helps us to more readily identify when we're projecting our own agenda onto other people. For example, it is absolutely vital to know when you're telling someone to not be in a relationship because you don't want to see them happy, versus when the spirit—the unconditioned vibration informing what you say—is actually making itself known. You need to be absolutely honest with yourself when you're doing the former.

For spirit workers, this is especially problematic, as speaking on behalf of an unseen entity comes with a certain gravity, a certain sense of authority not necessarily present in other interpersonal relations. Think about it: if you believe in spirits, and a medium tells you that a spirit wants you to break up with your partner, you might be more prone to taking such advice because, well, if a spirit said so, it must be true! In many cases it doesn't occur to the client or the medium that, really, it's the medium who can't handle you being in a relationship, not the spirit.

When we find ourselves in the position to share what we have received from spirits, it is our job to have first done enough personal work to be able to set aside our own personal agendas, as well as having a good sense of the kinds of voices that play on repeat in our monkey mind. Having done so, we will offer more sound counsel, more honest reflections, and find it relatively easy to answer the question, "Which of these voices in my head should I *not* be listening to right now?"

Chapter 6
Attunement Practices

The sections below describe practices that can help you become more sensitive to your immediate environment. This includes felt experiences in your body, as well as in the environment around you. I am intentionally not describing "how to contact spirits," because I believe that is something to be learned between a teacher and a student. Instead, what follows are a number of practices that can help re-sensitize you to your environment.

Hearing and Listening[58]

In spirit work, learning to hear is the ability to pick up what's being said amongst the chatter in our mind. It's the ability to differentiate between our inner monologue and the voice of spirit. Listening is the ability to stay with what's heard and comprehend what's being said.

There are a number of ways we can develop both our hearing and listening skills. Because hearing involves picking one thing out of many, we increase our hearing by tuning into a unique sound in our immediate environment.

You might find that amongst the sounds of the cars outside your window there are also people talking or birds chirping. Or, if you're in a park, behind you might be the sound of a squirrel running up a tree. Follow whatever sound catches your attention, and see if you notice anything unique about it. How does it distinguish itself? Is it soothing or grating on the ears? What sounds can you differentiate right now where you are? Pick one of these sounds. How does it differ from the others?

Listening involves comprehension. For example, hearing the sound of a bird off in the distance, focusing on it, and maintaining that focus for as long as you like. Letting the nuances of what makes the sound unique, teaches you something about the sound itself. What might the sound be communicating? Does it appear to be agitated? Is the sound hurried or more relaxed? Does the person speaking behind you sound happy or distressed? Does the sound of the air conditioner or heater sound labored, like it's been on for a while? Is the sound of the wind outside warning of a storm?

Quieting ourselves allows us to better appreciate the nuances of our surrounding environment, and shows us that there is much more going on than we might think.

Breathing Practices[59]

Most spiritual traditions have a number of breathing practices in their tool kit. Whether it's over-serving one's inhale and exhale, or more involved practices such as yogic *kapalabhati* breathing, working with the breath as a means to spiritual advancement is found all over the world.

Each breathing technique has a unique function. Some techniques are done primarily for the cleansing of the airways, others for the unblocking of energetic channels. Most breathing practices help clear the mind so as to induce a sense of calm and wellbeing in the practitioner.

Gently bringing your attention to your inhale and exhale is one of the quickest ways to initiate the so-called "quieting of our mind" that many spiritual practitioners are hoping to achieve.[60] As best you can, try breathing only through your nose, continuing to maintain attention as long as the inhale comes in, as well as for the duration of your exhale.

Gently focusing on our natural inhales and exhales, making a mental note of each, is one way to achieve a state of calm that also allows us to increase our awareness of our environment. When our attention is on the breath and not on our thoughts, the appearance of the world around us is enhanced.

Witness Meditation[61]

Witness meditation is the conscious effort of letting go of our identification with both our thoughts and emotions, as well as the external stimuli coming in through our senses. These three activities make up the majority of the chatter in our minds, and witness meditation allows us to observe these activities, rather than be pulled by them in various directions.

First, you want to come into a comfortable sitting position, or you may lay on your back. Begin following your natural breathing pattern as described in the previous section. From here you want to begin what spiritual teacher, Michael Singer, describes as leaning away from the thoughts, emotions, and sense perceptions that you are experiencing. These activities often feel as if they exist near the front of our head and face, and I have found it useful to imagine myself gently pulling back from this area of my body. As you do this, you may experience your thoughts as if they were passing images on a screen. This experience is the beginning stages of moving toward the seat of the witness.

Lectio Divina

Lectio divina, or engaged spiritual reading, is one of the oldest spiritual practices in the Catholic tradition, the origins of which date back to the 3rd century. The practice involves engaging with a passage from the Bible in four stages: reading, reflecting, responding, and contemplating. This helps guide the practitioner into greater intimacy with both the passage being read and the Spirit which informs it.[62]

First, find a passage you would like to read. You might pick a passage randomly and let chance decide where your engaged spiritual reading will take you, or, you could sit with a specific passage related to your interests, needs, or spiritual concerns. Take a few moments to come into a quiet mental state using either of the above practices or one of your own. Imagine opening yourself up to receiving divine inspiration.

Next, read the passage slowly either aloud or to yourself. Make a mental note of any words or phrases that catch your attention. This is the first step. Reading. You may read the passage more than once if you like.

Next, read the passage again, this time reflecting on both the overall meaning the passage has for you, as well as how the words or phrases that caught your attention relate to or inform this meaning. Lectio divina differs from scriptural analysis, but taking a few moments to appreciate how the language hits you can be very rewarding.

Then, read the passage again. Allow the passage to inspire you to respond in words. You may journal this response, or, as is traditionally recommended, come into prayerful communication with your Creator regarding what has come up for you.

In the final step you will read the passage

again, and come into a deep state of contemplation. Take as long as you like to sit silently, letting the experiences from the first three stages harness your attention on your love of God.

When you are finished, thank God and Spirit for the opportunity, and bring your awareness back into your body and the room.

The four practices above may be done on their own or together as a sequence leading up to lectio divina. The order they are listed in is intentional, and in my experience leads to a state of deep quiet.

Asking the Right Questions

> *Dear friends, do not believe every spirit, but test the spirits to see whether they are from God, because many false prophets have gone out into the world.*
> —1 John 4:1

In order to better prepare for inspired communication, we must first understand how and what our bodies are communicating to us. By engaging directly with the sensations in our body, asking it simple questions about what and how we feel, we can have profound insights into how our bodies communicate. At the same time this can bring us into a deep state of relaxation and sensitivity, the foundation of any spiritual practice designed to increase our experience of the world.

Whenever I feel as if there is something that needs to be communicated through my body, I get to know what it is by asking the following six questions:

1. How or what do I feel?[63]
2. Does this feeling have a shape?
3. Does this shape have a persona?
4. Does this persona have a voice?
5. What, if anything, does this voice have to say?
6. What does this voice need in order to be at peace?

1. How or what do you feel?

Spirit work is somatic work. Mediums and people sensitive to the presence of spirit regularly describe tingling sensations along their skin, light-headedness, or a weightiness on their shoulders. Feel into your body right now. Where are you experiencing a blockage or resistance? Are there areas that feel warm or cool? Do you have a sensation in your abdomen? Does it feel acidic and hot, cold and tight, or some other way entirely? Are there areas feeling pain? Are there areas that feel relaxed? If there is nothing noteworthy about your physical feeling state, return to your breath. Is it labored, shallow, deep, full, quick, or slow? Regardless of how pronounced or subtle the sensations are, know that you are living in a body. It feels things. What does it feel right now?

2. Does this feeling have a shape?

Maybe you have the sensation of a lump in your throat or a tingling sensation on the back of your neck. Does this feeling have a form? Does the lump in your throat feel round and thick or flat and square? What about the tingling sensation on your neck? Maybe it has the shape of a pinecone. Maybe it's shaped like a bat wing. What, if any, shape does your sensation have?

3. Does this shape have a persona?

What is the personality of this shape? Is it being aggressive or is it comforting? Does the knot in your stomach feel punishing or is it frustrated? Maybe it's bloated and lethargic. Maybe it's satiated and content. What about the lump in your throat? Is it proud and full of itself, struggling to get out and make itself known? Or, is it swaddled in a blanket, tired and wanting to be left alone? If this shape had a personality, is it one you'd like to be around?

4. Does this persona have a voice?

If this shape could talk, what might its voice sound like? Would it be high-pitched and grating on the ears, or low, deep, and resonant? What sounds does it make? Does it grunt or does it flutter? Maybe it sighs a lot. Maybe it whistles. Does it make a sound if it moves? Does it stomp around or flitter about? Maybe it hovers in silence.

5. What if anything does it have to say in this moment?

If you've made it this far, you're probably getting a good sense of what this presence feels like. You know there's a sensation associated with it. You know it has a shape, and a personality. You know what it sounds like when it opens its mouth or when it moves around your body. Now you'd like to know what it has to say to you. Three questions you might like to ask it are:

1. Why are you here?
2. What is your role in my life?
3. What are you trying to communicate?

Some of the most profound insights into the nature of my defenses and emotional patterns have been achieved by asking these three questions.

"Why are you here?" has given my emotional state an opportunity to be heard, to speak on its own behalf, and to tell me *in its own words* why it had surfaced in that given moment.

"What is your role in my life" has often led to an appreciation of the purpose a particular defense might have had in protecting me.

"What are you trying to communicate?" helps me enter into a dialogue with my emotional state, and explore why this experience is happening now.

6. What does this voice need in order to be at peace?

This question is a take on one of the questions from Tsultrim Allione's "Feeding your Demons" practice, which differentiates between asking what the entity *wants* versus what the entity *needs*. The difference is incredibly useful.

Allione deals in the world of demons as understood by the 12th century tantrika, Machig Labdrom. In response to asking the question, "What do you want?" Allione describes a "stress demon" who might reply "I want you to hurry up and get more done so you will be more successful." In response to the question "What do you need?" the same demon might respond by saying that it needs "to feel secure."[64]

What we want and what we need are usually two very different things. In times of duress we may want to have everyone around us go away. But, what we need may be more along the lines of comfort and understanding from someone we trust.

When working with spirit communication we sometimes find ourselves feeling off or unsettled by what we have been receiving. I recommend this last step as a way to recontextualize the experience you may be having. By finding out what the communication needs in order to feel safe and heard, we humanize and get to know aspects of ourselves that may be in need of a compassionate audience.

The main thing is to be non-combative. When it comes to defenses that inhibit us and difficult emotions that are bogging us down, there's often a desire to quickly get rid of them. We want to exorcise them. Cut them out of our life. We think we'd be better off without them. But, the truth is, while they may no longer be serving us now, in the past they served us quite well! They aren't going to let go just because we say so. Nor should they. Our defenses have served a purpose, and need to be both respected, and given a space to communicate.

WHEN ANSWERING the above questions it's important to remember that there are no right or wrong answers. The communication you receive might be incredibly eye opening, pertinent to a given situation, completely out of left field, comforting, or disturbing. The communication might even be funny, and you should feel free to laugh about what you experience. It's ok. This work can be very amusing!

Regardless of what comes up, you want to speak aloud. Speaking aloud makes it easier to tease out authentic communication from the tangled web of our own inner monologue.

Speaking aloud also helps bring the spirit into the room. I like to say that *the tongue is the bridge that spirits walk across.* Our own voice gives voice to the communication we're receiving. If we're in a group session, it allows the communication to interact with the rest of the group. In this way people's questions may be answered in more detail, or we may get to know the spirit on a more intimate level. After all, if a spirit is here, they are probably dealing with some unfinished business. As Florencio Guervara states above, it is part of our job to not only grow ourselves, but to elevate those who need upliftment. Speaking a spirit into the room gives us an opportunity to do both.

Speaking aloud also puts distance between ourselves and the communication, which is very important. Doing so reminds us that this is a received communication and not spirit possession. Spirit possession involves a person giving their body over to a spirit so as to provide the spirit with a vessel through which to express itself. Communicating with spirit, is exactly that: a communication between two beings. In spirit communication the beings do not merge. They speak to one another.

Mindful Rest

Wherever you end up at the end of this practice, it's important to take a few moments to rest and allow the experiences you had to integrate. You can do this sitting upright in a comfortable position or laying on your back. There is no need to follow your breath or do anything to make this more than it is. Simply rest. Three to five minutes should be sufficient.

A Note on Community and Therapy

The above practices are all safe things you can do to bring yourself into a quiet, open, and receptive state of being. While they can certainly be done in groups, most people find that setting aside time to be alone and practice greatly enhances one's ability to focus.

That said, I do not recommend doing any sustained spiritual practice in a vacuum. Whether it be spiritual practices like yoga, the study of scriptures, or engaging the spirit world, you need to learn from other people. Books are resources. They are not teachers. While you certainly don't need to run out and join a coven, move into an ashram, or become a nun, having a supportive community around you to bounce ideas and experiences off of is necessary for anyone who wants to build on solid ground. Think of your spiritual growth as pottery. In order for clay to hold water, it needs to be cooked. It needs to be fired in an oven. If not, it turns to mush everytime it gets handled. Engage with other people doing this work, and let others engage with the work you do.

Also, and I can't stress this strongly enough. If you have it within your means, find yourself a good therapist who is comfortable discussing your spiritual path. We all need living guides, mirrors, and sympathetic ears in order to grow, and it's a rare thing to have someone who can do all the above without any bias or personal agenda. Friends are great, but they are not therapists. Even your friends who happen to be therapists are not *your* therapist. If you intend to have any success unpacking the interior of your psyche so as to make yourself a better conduit of spirit, and especially one who doesn't project their own agenda onto other people, then you need a guide. And, a therapist can be a really great guide to have.

Chapter 7
Difficult Experiences

SPIRITUAL PRACTICE CAN BE DIFFICULT. If we come to it with hard and fast ideas about how it should feel or how it's supposed to look, we're setting ourselves up for immediate disappointment. The "spirit" in spirituality is confrontational. It's meant to disrupt our preconceived ideas, because preconceived ideas are created from within the confines of our limited perspective. And, there are no limits when it comes to Spirit.

Clinging to our own preconceived notions about who we think we are and how we're supposed to act in the world limits our ability to open up to new experiences. And yet, rejecting our natural limitations, causes us to clamp down even further. Spirit does not ask us to reject any part of ourselves. Spirit work is the practice of integration. If we're willing to open up to the presence of spirits, entities that exist in the shadows of our landscape, shouldn't we be allowed to open ourselves up to what exists in the shadows of our own psyche?

But, not everything that defines us is serving

our highest potential. We also recognize that aspects of our being can eventually run their course, and linger long past their expiration date. In order to subvert what no longer serves us without denying what makes us who we are, we need to try something a little different.

Acceptance and Allowance

> *Be kind to one another, tenderhearted, forgiving one another, as God in Christ forgave you.*
> —Ephesians 4:32

It would be unfortunate if what you took from the previous chapters was that the samskaras you've accumulated, and the voices of other people you've internalized, are in some way an error. Anyone who tells you that is gravely mistaken. The inner landscape, including the aspects that deserve examination, are the very aspects of ourselves that make us who we are. These are not things to get rid of. We are who we are in the world, *because* of our samskaras! They are aspects of our humanness to explore. So, the first aspect of opening up to spirit is to not judge what makes us who we are in the world.

Accept That You Have a Self

We don't want to judge the fact that we have a self that, at times, gets in the way of our expansion.

For far too long spiritual teachers have spoken harshly about what they call the "lower self," as if it is entirely burdensome in nature. One of the reasons why so many spiritual teachers end up being abusers and con artists is because they deny their "lower" self. They try to go around it. They ignore it. They have no praxis for refinement of the self, for teaching it to work on behalf of the greater good.

We do not deny our self in the work we're doing. We learn how to work with it. And, in so doing, we are able to experience more.

Allow Yourself and Others to be Wrong

My first experience of clamming up at Fernando's was not my last. Many times my teacher would try to get me to speak in our gatherings. I really wanted to speak, but felt too shy. My self would go into protection mode, not wanting me to extend beyond the safety of my perch. I only wanted to observe the work going on in the room. I was too scared to participate in it.

The spirit world can be a very busy place. Rooms can get crowded. It's important to know who has caught our ear. So, if you are planning on exploring the spirit world, don't be surprised if what comes to you is not useful to yourself or anyone else. In fact, the information you get may be flat out wrong. It may just be that you've picked up on something that isn't relevant right now.

Feeling Stuck

There are times when distinguishing between authentic messaging and the noise of a crowded mind can feel all but impossible. Many new spirit workers feel paralyzed in group sessions as they overthink their own experiences, worrying if what they are feeling warrants expression. This is incredibly common, and, in my opinion, a sign of maturity. Coming into a spiritual gathering assuming that everything you have to say will be God's word writ, is far more irresponsible than arriving with a bit of hesitancy.

Still, a spirit worker may become too cautious, unwilling to speak for fear that what they are feeling can't be trusted. It's hard enough to differentiate between the internalized voices of our childhood, let alone differentiate between those voices and the voices of spirits. Our mind is a very crowded place!

One way to circumvent the overwhelming chatter of the mind is to set aside your thoughts and feel into your body. Use the practices above to help bring your awareness back into your physicality. Then, start with what you feel. Your feeling state is often the most honest guide you have.

Uncomfortable Feelings

There may, however, be times when you don't feel comfortable with where the communication is headed. In these cases I again recommend following the advice of Florencio Guevara. If a spirit is felt too strongly, ask it to take three steps back.[65] You may then tell it to remove itself from the room, or, if you are willing to move forward with the session, begin interpreting the communication from this safer distance. Asking the spirit to take three steps back has the dual effect of maintaining healthy boundaries between self and other, and, for new practitioners, it creates a safe environment where the practitioner can slowly get to know the spirit.

Negative Thoughts

Negative thoughts can and do come up in this kind of work. And, it's easy to let our attention latch onto them and take us out of our center.

It's important to learn how to impose a sliver of distance between ourselves and these thoughts, many of which can be incredibly attractive to us, making it difficult to do so. We all know how easy it is to get wrapped up in the one negative thing a stranger says about us, rather than focus on the overwhelming amount of affirmation we get from those we love. Putting distance between ourselves and the thoughts gives us the perspective to see each thought as one of many passing by like clouds in the sky.

One of the most common ways to come into a healthy distance from our thoughts is to identify them. Whenever you find yourself stuck in a feedback loop of negativity, take a moment and label one of these particularly negative thoughts. *Thought about me not being cool enough.* Or, *Thought about me being a fraud.* When we label our thoughts, we begin witnessing our thoughts as they arise. They are not us. They are simply an expression of something we hold within us.

Over time we become skilled at recognizing the moments when we are attaching to the train of thoughts in our head, so much so that we begin to find it increasingly easy to simply back away from them. This practice of engaging with our negative thoughts aids in our ability to distinguish between what are our thoughts and what is inspired communication.

Spirit Possession

Spirit possession is a beautiful expression of the bridge that exists between the living and the dead. For me, witnessing spirit possession has been transformative in my appreciation and understanding of the interaction between spirit and humanity. Like anything worth doing well, it is a skill that requires guidance. It is something that needs to be learned from someone else.

For people just starting out, the experience of giving oneself over to another entity can be terrifying. It is for this reason that I do not give instructions on how to contact spirits, let alone "get possessed" in this book. All the mediums I have known have spent years honing their craft in close contact with an elder in the tradition within which they practiced. None of them learned on their own, and few if any spent much time reading books on the subject. Instead, mediums learn how to harness the spirit, through trial and error, and under the close watch of their guide.

In the groups that I sit with much of what we do is hold space for mediums to practice their craft. This is particularly important for new mediums who might still be learning how to navigate the presence of spirits.

During a possession a person may lose access to their own voice, speaking entirely on behalf of the spirit, and be unable to distinguish between themselves and the spirit possessing them. These are special circumstances, and are always voluntary. Rarely does a spirit enter a person in a space that has not been set up for that explicit purpose. In fact, even in cases where an unsolicited spirit forces itself into the room, these spirits are usually banished immediately.

New mediums often find it difficult to cede control over to the spirit, and thus lash out if the spirit is experienced as coming on too strong. Some believe that these wild displays of spirit possession are not necessarily indicative of the spirit's character, but a sign of the medium's resistance to the spirit's passing through them. In other words, a violent display of spirit possession does not necessarily indicate the presence of a violent spirit. The medium may get upset, angry, anxious or all the above. I have personally witnessed new mediums, overwhelmed by the passing of the spirit, screaming, clawing at their clothes, and throwing over unoccupied chairs in the room. In these instances it is the job of the senior mediums present to calm the spirit, or, in particularly difficult episodes, remove these entities from the space.

Because of this, any attempts to engage with inspired communication requires a larger-than-you-think display of humility. Jesus himself warns of what can happen when we don't respect the process of communicating with spirit:

> When the unclean spirit has gone out of a person, it passes through waterless places seeking rest, but finds none. Then it says, "I will return to my house from which I came." And when it comes, it finds the house empty, swept, and put in order. Then it goes and brings with it seven other spirits more evil than itself, and they enter and dwell there, and the last state of that person is worse than the first. So also will it be with this evil generation.[66]

This passage from the Gospel of Matthew details what's at stake when we forget to mind how we engage in this work, and become too comfortable or overly confident. The more we explore this work, the easier it will be to receive, interpret, and communicate messages from the spirits. Jesus warns about what can happen if we make ourselves available to unkind spirits by not tending to ourselves. We may think we have done all the work we need in order to open ourselves up to spirit communication, when in fact we have simply opened ourselves up to communication that will upset us.

Avoid shortcuts in all spiritual work that you do. Find a trustworthy teacher, and go slow. From there, all good things can happen. 🕯

Afterword

IN 2004 I WITNESSED MY FIRST POSSESSION.

I was traveling in Bahia, Brazil, living in the home of an elderly Candomblé priestess. One night, I accompanied my host to an initiation ceremony for new members of her religion.[67] With us were a number of students visiting from overseas. Neither them nor I had any idea what to expect.

During the ceremony, when the new initiates were embodying the dances of the *orixá* they had been crowed under, a young woman sitting in front of me, began flailing her body in every direction imaginable. I remember thinking she might dislocate her shoulders. Plastic white chairs went flying, and the elders monitoring the ceremony ran over in their white-frilled hoop skirts and head wraps, and quickly rushed our friend into the back room.

The next morning at breakfast, she was quiet. She didn't want to talk about what had happened, but mentioned that she would need to travel back to Bahia in a few months to finish what began the night before. Something about being "claimed" by one of the orixá. She was pensive, and chose her words carefully throughout the rest of the trip.

This book was written in honor of her experience, and all those who know what it feels like to stand at the intersection of the seen and the unseen. May those who cross the threshold be sweet with you always. 𓃭

Notes

1. Friedman, R.E., and Overton, S.D. (2000) Death and Afterlife: The Biblical Silence. *Judaism in Late Antiquity Part 4 Death, Life-After-Death, Resurrection & The World-to-Come in the Judaisms of Antiquity*, 35-59

2. Regarding "second coming prophetesses" see Francis, R. (2013). *Ann the Word: The Story of Ann Lee, Female Messiah, Mother of the Shakers*. New York, NY: Arcade Publishing.

3. When asked the question "Is religion important in your life?" 65% of Americans answered "yes." About 15% higher than Israel (51%), and about 20% lower than Iraq (84%). From a 2009 Gallup poll. For more information see https://news.gallup.com/poll/142727/religiosity-highest-world-poorest-nations.aspx

4. Delaney, B. (2017) The yoga industry is booming, but does it make you a better person? *The Guardian*. https://www.theguardian.com/lifeandstyle/2017/sep/17/yoga-better-person-lifestyle-exercise

5. Thistleton, AC. (2013). *The Holy Spirit—In Biblical Teaching, through the Centuries, and Today*. Grand Rapids, MI.: Wm. B. Eerdmans Publishing Co. p. 471

6. Ellicott, CJ. (1878) *A New Testament Commentary for English Readers, by Various Writers*. v. 2. New York, NY: Cassell, Petter, Galpin. p. 3

7. Acts 1:13

8. Acts 2:2–4

9. Luke 3:22

10. Acts 8:14–17

11. Mark 16:17

12. 2 Peter 1:21

13. For a history of Buddhism's introduction into Tibetan society, and the folk practices it encountered when it arrived, see *The Religions of Tibet*, by Giuseppe Tucci (1998).

14. 1 Corinthians 12

15. Caputo, JD. (2001). On Religion (Thinking in Action). New York, NY: Routledge. p. 33

16. Ibid.

17. Patanjali Yoga Sutras 3:37

18. Why might an increase in our physical and mental abilities, as granted by the spiritual efforts we have been making, be seen as dangerous to these same efforts? The answer may be found in understanding how we have allowed our society to be structured. Cultures based on hierarchy tend to disproportionately advantage those at the top by giving them greater access to resources (financial, natural, social, etc). Access to resources brings power, and power, in turn, provides access to more resources. From here the cycle repeats itself: power leading to access > leading to power > leading to access, *ad infinitum*. Not surprisingly, people who have power tend to want to hold onto it in order to keep the wheel spinning in their direction. In cultures where popularity leads directly to power and thus access, what quicker way to gain access to power than by stunning people with extraordinary abilities? Popularity is, at its root, the outcome of having the populous affirm your status as a powerful person. Miraculous powers are dangerous for those that acquire them, because they catapult people into the power-access-power hamster wheel. For more information on how power leads to an increased access to resources see Srilatha Batliwala & Lisa Veneklasen, "Social Exclusion and Access to Resources" (JASS-AWID Forum-2012).

19. Speciale, A. (2013). Are miracles really needed to become a saint? *RNS*. https://religionnews.com/2013/07/15/are-miracles-really-needed-to-become-a-saint/

20. While historically attributed to Paul, today 1 Timothy is believed to have been written by a different author at a later date.

21. Spiritual leaders within the Palo Mayombe religion, known as "tatas," will often consult with their *eggun*, literally, "the dead," when needing information.

22. Winkler, Rev. J. (2008). *Daily Meditations with the Holy Spirit*. NJ: Catholic Book Publishing Corp. p. 62

23. Matthew 8:28–32

24. Luke 4:33–35

25. Herbermann, C, ed. (1913). "Exorcism." *Catholic Encyclopedia*. New York, NY: Robert Appleton Company.

26. Mark 16:17–18

27. Burkert, W. (1985). *Greek Religion: Archaic and Classical*. Malden, MA: Harvard University Press. p. 180

28. Ibid, p. 180

29. Ibid, p. 331

30. Ibid, p. 332
31. *On the Vanity of Idols: Showing That the Idols Are Not Gods, and That God is One, and That Through Christ Salvation Is Given to Believers.* https://www.newadvent.org/fathers/050706.htm
32. Matthew 8:31
33. Mark 5:1–17
34. Patterson, S.J. (2014). *The Lost Way: How Two Forgotten Gospels Are Rewriting the Story of Christian Origins.* New York, NY: HarperCollins Publishers. p. 31–34
35. Khazan, O. (2018). Inherited Trauma Shapes Your Health. The Atlantic. https://www.theatlantic.com/ health/ archive/ 2018/ 10/ trauma-inherited-generations/573055/
36. May, R. (1969). *Love and Will.* New York City, NY: W.W. Norton & Company, Inc. p. 123
37. Ibid, p. 123
38. Ibid, p. 126
39. Jung, C. (1976). *Symbols of Transformation.* Princeton, NJ: Princeton University Press. p. 357
40. John 9:5–7
41. Luke 11:14
42. Mark 1:27
43. Allione, T. (2008). *Feeding Your Demons: Ancient Wisdom for Resolving Inner Conflict.* New York, NY: Little, Brown and Company.
44. Ibid.
45. There has been very little written about the mediums through which Kardec received the teachings, and upon which he later developed his spiritist philosophy. So much so is this the case, that Kardec is often thought to be the medium himself, when in fact he was the recorder of the spirit communications. The most well-known of Kardec's mediums was the somnambulist, Celine Japhet.
46. Kardec, A. (2008). *The Spirits' Book.* Brazil: International Spiritist Council. p. 140
47. Ibid, p. 141
48. Ibid, p. 146
49. Ibid, p. 147
50. Ibid, p. 149
51. Guevara, F. (2014). *Mesa Blanca.* Bloomington, IN: AuthorHouse. p. 12
52. We owe this term to the Buddhist teacher and psychothera-

pist, John Welwood. For a more indepth look at how spiritual bypass functions, see "Human Nature, Buddha Nature: An interview with John Welwood." *Tricycle: The Buddhist Review* (Spring 2011).

53. Genesis 2:7

54. The Sanskrit term "samskara" refers to "mental impressions" (Monier-Williams' Sanskrit-English Dictionary), and is a significant aspect of both Hindu and Buddhist philosophy. Michael Singer does an excellent job in his book *The Untethered Soul* (2007) of describing the samskaras and their effects on our thinking mind. My understanding of their function is largely indebted to that work.

55. Matthew 12:35

56. From https://www.blueletterbible.org/ (Lexicon :: Strong's G4190 - *ponēros*)

57. Matthew 12:34

58. The Quakers are known for their teachings on listening, and one would do well to seek those out, if interested in going further into this practice. Mallorie Vaudoise's book *Honoring Your Ancestors: A Guide to Ancestral Veneration* (2019) offers a number of practices for learning how to become sensitive to your environment. Her inclusion of the Situationist practice of psychogeographic walking is particularly great.

59. There are enumerable books on yogic breathing practices known as *pranayama*, although each will, correctly in my opinion, recommend that you find a teacher. For a brief introduction to breathwork from a non-yogic perspective that includes a number of practices you can do on your own, see Jennifer Patterson's T*he Power of Breathwork: Simple Practices to Promote Wellbeing*, (2020).

60. Of course, we never really quiet our mind, because our mind is not necessarily under our control. What we do achieve, however, is a state where our focus is on something other than the inner monologue constantly going on in the background, which in turn has the effect of calming us down.

61. Here I am, once again, indebted to Michael Singer's book *The Untethered Soul*. While by no means a replica, my practice of witness meditation is heavily informed by Singer's teachings.

62. 1 Corinthians 2:9–10

63. Questions 1-5 are based on techniques I have used in sessions with a somatic psychotherapist over the course of ten years.

Typically, they are meant to help the client place a sliver of distance between themselves and their emotional state in an effort to help the client experience the emotion more fully, rather than merge with it. The difference having the ability to clearly convey the emotional experience you are having in words (i.e. "I am feeling really angry right now"), versus lashing out from an angry place.

64. *Feeding Your Demons* (2008), p. 62–3
65. *Mesa Blanca* (2014), p. 28
66. Matthew 12:43–45
67. With the exception of one night, week-long ceremonies for new initiates are closed to the public.

For those who find themselves standing
at curious intersections.

Appendix A

Wild Christianity: A Manifesto for the Reclaiming of One's Root Religion

Each generation...rescues a new area from what its predecessors arrogantly and snobbishly dismissed as "lunatic fringe."
—Christopher Hill, *The World Turned Upside Down*

FOR YEARS, many of us who were born into the Christ tradition have looked outside our family's religious lineage in order to find homes that would satisfy our curiosities. As the spiritual teacher, Ram Dass, has said, we needed to find people who had the "maps of consciousness,"[1] people who had a spiritual worldview big enough to include our wild ways, our impatient seeking, our counter-cultural mores. Catholicism and Christianity had let us down in almost every way imaginable, and, as spiritual exiles, we needed to find people to take us in.

We traveled far and wide to find religious expressions that matched how we wanted our spirituality to look and feel. In many cases we found people who were more than willing to open their doors. Buddhist monks adopted us. Hindu sadhu babas adopted us. In some cases lineage holders of the very spiritual traditions and cultures our ancestors fought so hard to destroy—Native People traditions, African traditions—even *they* adopted us.

Throughout our mass exodus, the religion we were born into had continued to wreak havoc on the world through its pursuit of cultural dominance. Perhaps we thought that by dissolving our identification with the Christ tradition we would somehow create an irreparable vacuum that would suck the life out of the religious behemoth we were rebelling against. Instead we took our eyes off the enemy, while at the same time it refined its attacks, moving farther to the right, and seeped deeper into the political agendas of the State.

We tried to shirk responsibility by claiming that we no longer had anything to do with the religious institutions of our parents. *It's them, not us. We've rejected our parents' religious path.* Identifying with religious expressions outside our cultural upbringing, we thought we were free from criticism.

In the most noble of cases we sat at the feet of gurus, monks, and shamans soaking up as much of their wisdom as we could. Rarely did we convert to the religions upon which our new teachers' spiritual teachings were founded. (For example, few western Ganesh worshippers actually converted to Hinduism). Nor did we fully immerse ourselves into the culture these teachers came from. (Rare were those who spent time in a Japanese Zen temple only to never leave). Nevertheless, we felt as if we had made some sort of transition out of our parents' conservative ways and into something new. The best of us learned from and helped support our new teachers, promoting their messages to others, while at the same time trying to act and behave as righteous emissaries of the exotic.

In worst cases we merely donned the affects of the religious traditions we tried to identify with. We turned their cultural wares into costumes, substitute skins we could shed whenever we encountered unfriendly territory at work or in the suburbs. Whether acting in good faith or as a spiritual tourist, there was often a sense that even though we felt as outsiders in our family's root religion, we were still somehow outside this new, more exotic one. Whispered accusations of cultural appropriation began to waft through the air, and we all huddled under our sheets hoping no one would notice our sometimes less-than-honest intentions. Always ready to point the finger at someone else whom we felt was less genuine than we.

Some people pushed back against accusations of cultural appropriation—believing it simply to be an unfortunate side effect of globalization done in bad taste—that the reason it had become so controversial a subject was because it was offensive to cultural natives. (It's no wonder the accused continue to find this reasoning hard to accept. In North America, freedom of expression must be upheld even in cases of extreme offense. And, rightly so).

However, cultural appropriation is not an issue because it offends people. It's an issue, because, as Native American rights activist, Ward Churchill, has said, cultural appropriation is an avoidance of responsibility. It's an attempt to "sidestep" the controversial heritage people are a part of, rather than "putting it back in balance." Avoiding responsibility allows people to "pretend to be other than who and what they are."[2] It gives people an excuse to avoid looking at their own stake in the oppression of other people.

Therefore, it is time, spiritual exiles, those who have been cast out, and those who have willingly and understandably cast away their spiritual root tradition. It is time to turn our attention back in on ourselves. It is time to reclaim, reexamine, reinterpret, and repair the religions of our ancestors. It is finally time to clean up our own backyards, and make peace with where we have come from.

•

BY TURNING TOWARD THE RELIGION of our upbringing we intend to steal back the mystical, folksy, anarchic Christ tradition from the fascists and the fundamentalists.

Together we must uncover the radical aspects of this vast and varied spiritual tradition. We must step outside the canon of acceptable religious ideas and norms, and jump head first into the margins. When we get there, we're going to meet fascinating, and, at times, unruly characters—non-conformists with wild ideas, anti-authoritarians with antinomian practices—the spirits of whom we will escort back across the thinly veiled threshold that separates the living from the dead.

In many ways it will be easy to get the ball rolling. The Christ tradition is over two thousand years old, and throughout that time has been host to enumerable rabble rousers, free thinkers, freedom fighters, and miscreants. All we need to do is start scratching the surface.

•

THE MOVEMENT to reclaim the Christ tradition is for anyone who's ever found themselves rejecting their Catholic or Christian roots, because the religion felt far too conservative and intolerant. It's a movement for people who find themselves standing at non-normative intersections. It's a movement for people who might find themselves enamored with the primordial Christ within all beings, but also embracing the witchy ways of old. It's for people who might venerate saints while attending Quaker meetings; who might channel helpful spirits, while casting out those that require too much of their attention; who might loath "Christian Rock" cuz it's the worst, but love Jamaican dub cuz it's the best; who might never exclaim "Praise, Jesus!" in the way the born-agains do, cuz it sounds really born again-y, and, like, this isn't about being a good Bible beating Christian, or anything. But, it's also for people who might still really dig the "Anointed One." It's a movement for people who might liberally explore all sorts of spiritual practices, and who might make some up; who might never refer to themselves as "Christian," cuz the jerks and the fascists and the full-of-hate conservative right-wingers and their limited vision have completely ruined the term. But, it's also for people who might!

This movement is for people like you and me who at some point on our spiritual journey decided that we were tired of having to choose between this sect or that denomination—trying to fit our circle peg selves into square holes. Instead, we want access to the *entirety* of the Christ tradition!

We want:

- The ritual and pomp of Catholicism
- The practical magic of our folk traditions
- The direct mystical experience—aka the gnosis—of the Gnostics

- The anti-establishment of the early Protestants
- The simple egalitarianism of the Quakers
- The herbalism and ecstasy of the Shakers
- The enrapturing of the Pentecostals
- The big beautiful musical noise of the Baptists
- The social justice of liberation theologists
- The natural livity and radical interpretations of the Rastafarians
- The kitchen witchery of Italian nanas
- The root-work and fuck-the-master resiliency of the African diaspora (and to never forget they were brought to America as slaves, and if you're white you gotta get real with that)
- The skillful and playful syncretisms of Latin America
- The shape-shifting gender nonconformity of the Corinthians
- The autonomy and audacity of the hippie communes
- The antinomianism of the Ranters
- The anarcho-socialism of the Diggers
- The mystery of the Adamites

And, leave all the BS behind!

No longer will we allow the seemingly separate entities comprising the far-right, Christian right, alt-right, neo-fascist nationalist movements, white racialists, nativists, and religious fundamentalists—all of whom comprise the seven heads of the Leviathan—to dominate the discussion about what it means to be a participant in the Biblical tradition. For, as it is written, the Leviathan is destined to be smashed to bits by the

Divine, and fed to the people of the wilderness.[3] And, we are those People.

We're going to become, in the words of the poet, Bruce Andrews, "wild readers" of our tradition,[4] ready to devour the Leviathan of fascistic readings and interpretations. We will employ what poet and critical theorist, Juliana Spahr, has called "anarchic reading," a way of engaging with texts and narratives that "value an elasticity of responses."[5] We will crack open the language that has been used to construct the major concepts of the Christ tradition. We will think creatively on histories, concepts, and ideas that have hitherto been interpreted as a means to centralize authority.

For, we are the ones who exist outside the centralized authority of Christianity. We are the ones who, like wild growth, believe in the power of rhizomatic decentralized communities of seekers working together. We are the ones who look to wild ways for insight. We are the ones who heal the sick with what is produced from God's earth. We are the ones who want food made from what grows in the ground. We are the ones who have been wandering the spiritual borderlands for years looking for sustenance.

IT IS TIME TO SHOW YOURSELVES, People of the Wilderness, feral beasts, wild souls living in human bodies. Animals—ALL OF US—rooting out authentic religious experiences like truffles in the slop. It is time to come out of the woods, down from the mountain, and see what has been taking place on the plains.

It is time, People of the Wilderness. It is time to steal back our Wild Christianity.

Notes

1. Lemle, M. (Producer and Director). (2001). *Fierce Grace* [Motion Picture]. United States: Zeitgeist Films.
2. Jensen, D. (2004). *Listening to the Land: Conversations about Nature, Culture, and Eros*. White River Junction, VT: Chelsea Green Publishing Company. p. 160
3. Psalm 74:14
4. Andrews, B. (1995). *Paradise and Method: Poetry and Praxis*. Evanston, IL: Northwestern University Press. p. 54
5. Spahr, J. (2001). *Everybody's Autonomy: Connective Reading and Collective Identity*. Tuscaloosa, AL: The University of Alabama Press. p. 155

Appendix B
Chaplet of the Seven Gifts

IN 1895, Pope Leo XIII asked all Catholics to pray for the Holy Spirit to enter and "renew the world." Answering this call was Blessed Elena Guerra, known affectionately as "the Holy Spirit Apostle of modern times," who in 1896 composed invocations asking the Holy Spirit to bless the world with a "New Pentecost." Guerra based her chaplet on the seven gifts of the Holy Spirit as outlined in Isaiah 11:2–3.

What follows is an adaptation of Guerra's Chaplet to the Holy Spirit, which replaces the gifts from Isaiah 11 with those mentioned in 1 Corinthians covered earlier in this book. As there are a number of different "Holy Ghost" chaplets in the Catholic tradition, I have made this change not to take away from Guerra's composition, which is wonderful in its own right, but to add to the diversity of Holy Spirit invocations. The *charismata* mentioned by Paul are unique, having a certain immediacy to them. This, I believe, makes them deserving of their own prayers.

May this chaplet bring you great joy and spiritual guidance.

You may use any rosary (or chaplet), containing seven large beads separated by seven smaller beads. On each large bead ask the Holy Spirit to offer Her gifts to you. Feel free to elaborate on the petitions below. On the seven smaller beads pray "Father, in the Name of Jesus, send forth your Spirit and renew the world," followed by one "Mary, Mother of God, who by the work of the Holy Spirit, conceived the Savior, pray for us."

The Chaplet of the Seven Gifts

Glory be to the Father, the Son, and the Holy Spirit. As it was in the beginning, is now, and forever shall be, world without end. Amen.

First Mystery: The Gift of Wisdom and Knowledge
Most High Holy Spirit, who brings Wisdom and Knowledge, help me to have clarity when I am unsure.

7x: "Father, in the Name of Jesus, send forth your Spirit and renew the world."
1x: "Mary, Mother of God, who by the work of the Holy Spirit, conceived the Savior, pray for us."

Second Mystery: The Gift of Faith
Most High Holy Spirit, who brings Faith, help me to take comfort in the unknown.

7x: "Father, in the Name of Jesus..."
1x: "Mary, Mother of God..."

Third Mystery: The Gift of Healing
Most High Holy Spirit, who brings the Power to Heal, help me to undo the sickness that binds myself and others.

7x: "Father, in the Name of Jesus..."
1x: "Mary, Mother of God..."

Fourth Mystery: The Gift of Miraculous Powers
Most High Holy Spirit, who brings Extraordinary Abilities, help me to expand the limits of what we believe is possible in God's world through my actions.

7x: "Father, in the Name of Jesus..."
1x: "Mary, Mother of God..."

Fifth Mystery: The Gift of Prophecy
Most High Holy Spirit, who brings the Gift of Prophecy, help me to see what lies ahead, and guide me through unforseen troubles.

7x: "Father, in the Name of Jesus..."
1x: "Mary, Mother of God..."

Sixth Mystery: The Gift of Having the Ability to Distinguish Between Spirits
Most High Holy Spirit, who brings the Ability to Distinguish Between Spirits, help me to discern between the

forces that benefit me and those that lead me astray.

7x: "Father, in the Name of Jesus..."
1x: "Mary, Mother of God..."

Seventh Mystery: The Gift of Speaking in Tongues and Interpreting Tongues
Most High Holy Spirit, who brings the Gift of Tongues, help me to speak authentically on your behalf, and to have wisdom to interpret your messages in whatever form they come.

7x: "Father, in the Name of Jesus..."
1x: "Mary, Mother of God..."

Invocation to Mary

O most pure Virgin Mary, by your Immaculate Conception you were made a chosen tabernacle of Divinity by the Holy Spirit. Pray for us.

May the Divine Paraclete come soon to renew the face of the earth.

Hail, Mary, full of grace, the Lord is with thee. Blessed are you among women, and blessed is the fruit of your womb. Holy Mary, Mother of God, pray for us who miss the mark, now and at the hour of our death. Amen.

O most pure Virgin Mary, by the Mystery of the Incarnation you became true Mother of God by the Holy Spirit. Pray for us.

May the Divine Paraclete come soon to renew the face of the earth.

Hail, Mary...

O most pure Virgin Mary, persevering in prayer with the Apostles in the Upper Room, you were abundantly inflamed by the Holy Spirit. Pray for us:

May the Divine Paraclete come soon to renew the face of the earth.

Hail, Mary...

Send Your Spirit, Lord, and transform us interiorly with Your gifts. Create in us a new heart that we may please You and be conformed to Your will. Through Christ our Lord. Amen.

Biblical Quotes: *This book contains a number of quoted passages from the* Bible. *Most of these are from the* New International Version, New Living Translation, *or* English Standard Version *editions. When quoting the Book of Sirach, or other books found only in Catholic editions, I referenced both* The Good News Translation, *as well as the* Revised Standard Version–Catholic Edition. *These translations, like all translations, are not entirely to my liking. In each instance, I chose whichever translation I felt was easiest to understand, and, when appropriate, offered gender-neutral pronouns. In very few instances I made small edits for clarity. As a rule, I have no allegiance to any one translation, and feel no obligation to stick to a single translation when quoting the* Bible *in my writing. I recommend this practice to anyone who wishes to have a better appreciation of* The Good Book.

Diacritcal Marks: *On the whole I did not include diacritical marks in non-English words. Those that were familiar to me, or are in common usage, I chose to keep. Öthers I left öüt.*

Answer page 11: *SWISS*